YOU *ARE* ALLOWED

YOU *ARE* ALLOWED

A Story of Finding Where You Belong, Not Where You Began

ODELIA ELGARAT

DANS LA LUNE
Highlands Ranch, Colorado

YOU ARE ALLOWED
by Odelia Elgarat

Published by

DANS LA LUNE

Dans la lune – Publishing LLC
Highlands Ranch, Colorado
www.odeliaelgarat.com

Editing by Sheral DeVaughn
Cover Art by Danielle Elgarat
Book Design by Nick Z, Journey Bound Publishing

ISBN: 979-8-9901128-0-3 (Paperback)
ISBN: 979-8-9901128-1-0 (EBook)
Library of Congress Control Number: 2024908885

Second Edition
Printed in the United States of America

Contents

Dedications

To my dear Mother,

*I*n the profound journey of introspection and self-discovery that spanned nine years through the art of writing, I learned more about my mother than I could have imagined. I unearthed the complex layers of my mother's character, revealing her to be an extraordinary feminist figure. As I delved into the recesses of my memories, I came to recognize the remarkable strength that defined her decision to embrace me and to adopt me into the warm folds of her love.

It is with a deep sense of gratitude and reverence that I acknowledge the pivotal role she played in shaping the course of my life. Reflecting on the trajectory of our relationship, I consider myself incredibly fortunate that she, with her boundless love and compassionate heart, chose me as her own and undertook the noble responsibility of caring for me. Her decision, a testament to her unwavering courage and compassion, has left an indelible mark on the canvas of my existence.

Her wise and invaluable teachings have been my guiding light through the labyrinth of life's challenges. I have carried them with me as a source of strength and wisdom. I have drawn upon them when faced with the myriad trials and tribulations that have unfolded in life. Her resilience, unwavering commitment to justice, and unyielding spirit have inspired me to stand tall in the face of adversity. She taught me the power of determination and perseverance.

As I pen these words, I am filled with a deep sense of gratitude for the love, wisdom, and strength she has given to me. Every lesson, every piece of advice, and every act of love has been etched into the fabric of my being, shaping me into the person I am today.

So, from the depths of my heart, I extend my heartfelt gratitude to you, Mom. Thank you for being the embodiment of strength, love, and resilience. Thank you for choosing me and showering me with the warmth of your embrace. I am forever indebted to you for the immeasurable impact you have had on my life.

With love and gratitude,

Odelia, your first baby forever.

To my birth mother, Yvette,

I want to express my deepest gratitude to you for bringing me into this world. Without your strength and love, I wouldn't have the gift of life. Thank you for enduring the pregnancy and the delivery. I can only imagine how challenging it must have been for you.

Your decision to place me for adoption was incredibly courageous, and it's a decision that has shaped my life in profound ways. Because of your selflessness, I had the opportunity to be raised by wonderful parents and to have a sister who means the world to me. I am the woman I am today because of your brave choice.

Our journey hasn't been easy for either of us. Yet, I feel incredibly fortunate that we had the chance to meet, even if it was just once, 14 years ago. That short reunion meant the world to me. I am grateful for the glimpse into your life that you shared with me. It was during that time that I saw how much we resemble each other, which fills my heart with a sense of connection and belonging.

As I come to the end of my writing journey, I find peace knowing that I've had the opportunity to express my gratitude and love to you. I hope that you, too, have found peace and happiness in your life.

Yvette, I wish I had the chance to say these words to you sooner: I love you.

With all my heart,

Odelia, your last baby forever.

Chapter 1

The Announcement

Western Negev, Israel | January 2014

The red numbers on the alarm clock read 6:00 am, flickering against the black background.

He reached over to turn off the alarm, leaning in gently to leave a soft mint-scented kiss on her forehead. "Good morning," he whispered, a tender greeting to start the day. She stirred from her slumber, her eyes searching for his presence.

"When did you get up?" she inquired, the morning haze still lingering in her voice.

He smiled, a hint of mischief in his eyes. "A long time ago. I'm already on my way out. Will you talk to your parents today?" he asked, his words carrying a sense of anticipation. He stared at her with his soft green eyes.

"I'll try," she replied, a mixture of both determination and uncertainty in her response.

As he opened the window, the morning light flooded into the room, temporarily blinding her as he prepared for the day. The lingering scent of rain from the night before enveloped the air like a heavy perfume, adding a touch of nostalgia to the morning atmosphere.

"I'm leaving for work now, but I'll see you this evening. Love you." he said before heading out.

Esther reluctantly left the warmth of her bed. It was time to wake up her four children. She tiptoed into her teen son's room, whispering a soft, "Good morning. It's time to get up and get ready for school, Sweetie."

The routine repeated in her eldest daughter's room. It was a morning ceremony filled with maternal care and love.

The day unfolded in the kitchen. Esther prepared a delightful breakfast for her children. Toasted bread with butter and jam evoked nostalgic memories of her own childhood, reminiscent of when she was a little girl.

Occasionally, the strawberry jam gave way to Nutella, adding a sweet twist to the morning ritual. An array of cookies, often featuring smiley faced designs with chocolate or vanilla nestled between the two layers, always graced her table.

In her youth, Esther's mom would lovingly prepare hot chocolate milk for her, wrapping her in delicious warmth and comfort. Now, as a mother herself, she adapted the morning tradition to coffee or tea for her own children. She was creating new moments of warm memories and continuing a cherished tradition that she carried with her since her early years.

Her eldest daughter joined her, skillfully assisting in the making of coffee. It added an extra layer of connection and generational bonding to the morning routine.

"Take your lunch and a snack. And don't forget your water bottle," Esther reminded both teens. It was the routine of a mother ensuring her children were ready for the day ahead.

"Have a good day," Esther called after them, her voice carrying a mix of love and encouragement as they closed the door behind them on their way to the bus station.

Now it was time to make lunch boxes for the little ones and get them ready for the day. It was a routine that Esther approached with both love and efficiency.

"Good morning, cuties," she said softly as she entered their dark little room. There she lingered, hugging and kissing each child until they gradually stirred from their sleep. Esther carefully selected their clothes from the closet and helped them get dressed, taking a moment to brush their fine blonde hair with maternal tenderness.

After a satisfying breakfast, she reminded them, "Don't forget to brush your teeth and wash your cute faces!" Following the morning routine, the little ones put on their shoes and shouldered their heavy backpacks, preparing for the day ahead. With a swift motion, Esther closed the door behind her, clutching her children's hands in each of hers, and descended the familiar path of their yard. A bright ray of sunlight pierced through the white clouds overhead. On their way to the bus stop, they passed unassuming square houses much like their own.

"Hurry up, hurry up," she instructed the children, aware of the impending arrival of the bus. Pearls of sweat formed on Esther's back as she looked down at the little girl's worried face. Punctuality was crucial for her.

The silence that enveloped the *kibbutz* during the night had dissipated, replaced by the bustling sounds of kids coming from various paths and spreading throughout the *kibbutz*. They were like small brooks of people converging and spilling into the sea of the bus station.

While Esther occasionally sat with her children at the station amongst the other *kibbutz* youngsters, this morning they arrived at the same time as the white bus. The head of security, a constant presence in light jeans and a T-shirt, carried his M16 rifle on his back, resembling a turtle with its shell.

"First grade is first up," he announced. It was a daily routine that signaled the commencement of the school day. Esther drew her youngest son into a warm embrace before he settled on the pavement, observing his sister climbing confidently up the bus stairs to take her seat by the window. Standing on the sidewalk, Esther waved with a forced smile as the bus disappeared behind the *kibbutz's* yellow gate. Her son began to cry, causing Esther to contemplate the option of taking him to kindergarten in the car. She decided against it. The doctor had emphasized the importance of exercise.

"Look," she said to her son and pointed to plants as they walked along the *kibbutz* paths. "That's eucalyptus. That's pine. And these are what? Chrysanthemums." She paused in front of each of them, occasionally caressing the leaves with her hands.

She recalled her father's teachings during her own childhood. As she named the plants, the nostalgia of those moments filled her thoughts. She remembered the scent of her oversized, green garden boots. Her father had given them to her to work with him in their backyard every Saturday in France when she was a girl. Over the years, she had worn them during countless gardening sessions.

Meanwhile, the boy ran ahead, jumping gleefully into a puddle. The sight snapped her back to the present.

Upon reaching the kindergarten schoolyard, they crossed through and entered the modest, but new building. Esther and her son knelt beside a little table. Quietly they began their shared activity of putting together a puzzle.

"Well," she finally said, breaking the silence. "Mommy has to go. But I'll be back soon, as always." She hugged her son tightly, checking his little blue eyes to ensure he was fine.

On her way out, she approached the kindergarten assistant. "Chantal, hug him," she pleaded, leaving behind a sense of assurance for her youngest before continuing with the rhythm of the day.

Esther closed the kindergarten gate behind her, the metallic clink echoing in the air, and turned to make her way to the grocery store.

As she pulled at the rectangular iron handle of the glass store door it refused to budge. Esther pulled harder; her frustration evident. The door remained firmly closed, mocking her attempts. Shielding her eyes with both hands from the sun's glare, she peered inside, only to find the store empty. A sigh escaped her lips. She considered the idea of returning home and trying again later. The slump of her shoulders revealed her fatigue.

She looked around, her gaze drifted to a stack of newspapers neatly arranged on a narrow brown bench beneath an expansive wooden pergola. She sat on the bench and picked up the newspapers. She began reading the big and colorful headlines that promised some good news. She skipped over the sports page and checked the weather.

Just then, Claudio, the store manager, emerged from the trees. His keys jingled noisily in his hand as he looked at her. "I can't believe it," he muttered. "She will not leave." Esther let go of the newspapers and looked at him, smiling.

Claudio, still muttering under his breath, walked past her and inserted a key into the grocery store lock. He twisted it around, and with a decisive pull, the transparent doorknob turned.

"Good morning, come in Esther!" he exclaimed, motioning for her to hurry. "Quickly, before any more mothers see you and want to come for some milk, too."

Esther managed a grateful, "Good morning, Claudio. Thank you."

As they stepped inside, Esther couldn't help but notice Claudio's dense beard hair. She was fascinated with the contrast of his thin frame and the size of his beard. She couldn't help but wonder how he managed not to tip over with such a substantial beard on his slender body.

She was on a covert mission, sensing an almost clandestine aura as if she had just breached a concealed entrance to access the store. Claudio, catching her scrutinizing the door entry point, furrowed his forehead.

"Hurry, Esther," he urged as she stepped into the small and dimly lit store. The modest grocery store, adorned only with a handful of baskets and devoid of any carts, unfurled itself for her early morning shopping ritual.

"Milk, bread, milk, bread," Esther whispered to herself, a mantra to ensure she forgot nothing. She made her way to the refrigerator near the entrance, selecting a milk carton beside the cottage cheese and margarine, double-checking the expiration date.

As she made her way to the bread section, she passed an open door leading to the back room. There was Haim, weary from unloading crates of merchandise. He sent her a tired glance.

Stopping in front of a little freezer, Esther indulged a childish guilt and grabbed a container of chocolate ice cream.

"1750," she announced to Claudio as she approached the cash register, placing the groceries on the shiny, cold iron surface.

"I remember your number, Esther," Claudio said with a grin, his Argentinian accent adding a touch of unfamiliar warmth to her name.

"Thank you, Claudio. Thank you very much," she replied, inexplicably blushing. "You saved me."

"You are welcome," he replied, his gaze lingering a moment longer.

Esther made her way to the door while Claudio followed quietly. As she stepped outside, leaving her smile within the store, Claudio locked the door behind her back. She knew he would head back through the merchandise door to join Haim on the concrete ramp for black coffee and a cigarette. Though she would be an uninvited guest, Esther harbored a secret desire to join in the camaraderie she observed from afar.

On her way home, Esther strolled past the familiar landmarks of the *kibbutz,* each holding its own story within the fabric of daily life.

She sauntered past the laundromat, where the hum of washing machines blended with the rhythmic beats of community living.

The clubhouse, a hub of social gatherings and shared moments, stood as a testament to the camaraderie that defined the *kibbutz* experience.

Next to it were a pair of secretarial buildings, conjoined twins that seemed to have been born with the very essence of the *kibbutz* itself. They were witnesses to the ebb and flow of communal existence.

As she continued on the path, Marco's voice rang out from the doorway of the sewing shop.

"Esther! ¿Qué pasa?" he called out, a warm greeting that echoed through the *kibbutz* air. Esther's face lit up with a smile as she acknowledged him.

On the other side, Rosa, perched on the dining room stairs, waved enthusiastically, creating a sense of connectedness in the tight-knit community. Esther waved back, fostering the communal spirit that permeated the *kibbutz*.

Passing the dining room's heavy glass door, Esther felt a sudden pang of hunger. Thoughts of the ice cream nestled in the plastic bag surfaced. She sighed, contemplating the temptation that lay within. The morning had only just begun, yet she realized she was on the verge of breaking her diet. She deliberated on whether to discard the tempting treat as she continued her stroll.

Finding a bench next to the old playground, Esther took a seat. Her gaze lingered on the faded plastic equipment that bore the marks of countless summers basking in the slow rise of the *kibbutz* sun. A vibrant red hibiscus flower fell delicately at her feet. It was a small, yet poignant reminder of the beauty embedded in the everyday moments of *kibbutz* life. She rose and continued her journey; the flower serving as a fleeting companion in her path.

Passing her neighbor Shelly's house, Esther couldn't resist stealing a glance, hoping to catch a glimpse of her in the backyard. Recollections of the day when Shelly had invited her to share a cigarette after she first moved into the *kibbutz* lingered in Esther's memory. Since then, she had quietly yearned for a repeat of that invitation, an insignificant gesture that held the promise of friendship and connection. Shelly hadn't invited her again, but Esther remained hopeful.

A glance at her watch revealed it was 8:30 am. Her mom would be calling any minute. The anticipation of the phone call added a sense of structure to Esther's meandering journey, weaving her personal narrative into the fabric of the *kibbutz's* collective story.

She continued her journey back home through the parking lot that separated the original *Kibbutz Mefalsim*. It was established in 1949 in the northwest Negev desert by immigrants from Argentina and Uruguay. Shelly's mom had once explained to her that the name "Mefalsim" translated to "clearing a path." It symbolized the Latin American immigrants who paved the way for others to make *Aliyah*. They were proud. Esther crossed the parking lot and strolled beside the small new playground.

On the opposite side of the parking lot lay the extension neighborhood, where Esther lived with her family in a rented house. *Kibbutz Mefalsim* was a trailblazer, pioneering the construction of an extension neighborhood and welcoming new members. It set a precedent for other *kibbutzim*. A member once explained to her that this transformative initiative marked a significant shift in *kibbutz* society.

A new parking lot, a fresh playground, newly planted trees, new houses, and unfamiliar faces—these elements, not belonging to the core *kibbutz* community, served as both dividers and links between the old and the new. In some ways, they acted as a bridge, offering a glimmer of hope. Yet their presence appeared somewhat unnatural against the backdrop of the Negev's rugged and untamed nature.

She put her hand on the handle and opened the door of the house. At the *kibbutz*, people didn't lock doors. That was the tradition, a communal trust ingrained in the rhythm of daily life. Esther, however, couldn't embrace this practice entirely. Every time she left the house, a fear of potential burglars lingered in her mind. Still, she mused, it is the *kibbutz* family custom, a testament to the unique blend of communal living.

Esther placed the milk in the refrigerator upon entering her home. Before stashing the ice cream in the freezer, she indulged in a few spoonfuls. It was a guilty pleasure she couldn't resist. All she wanted now was the simplicity of coffee and a cigarette. They provided her immense comfort.

Before she could enjoy them, a list of chores loomed in front of her. Washing dishes, tidying the children's beds, starting the washing machine, and perhaps mopping the floor. In her imagination a fictional policeman stood in front of her. He was a stern figure urging her to engage in the daily chores.

She diligently picked up toys scattered across the floor, creating an orderly space for her children. Returning to the kitchen, she stood by the sink, gazing out the window at the palm branches swaying in the wind. The silence enveloped her like a whisper, prompting her to turn on the radio for company. Melodious tunes filled the air, momentarily breaking the stillness. "*Who walks by my side through the journey, with every dream, with every look...?"* The lyrics played, and Esther, lost in thought, turned off the radio. She didn't let the singer finish the sentence. She didn't want to hear that word—*"Mom."*

She set the kettle on the stove, starting the routine of her morning tasks. As the water boiled, she went to her bedroom to make her bed. It was another of her familiar chores that marked the beginning of each day.

Returning to the kitchen, she retrieved her preferred mug and set it on the counter. She picked up the phone to call Nava and then Nofit. She wanted companionship, but no one answered. A tinge of sadness crossed her heart, yet the aroma of coffee lifted her spirits.

"How much sugar today? Four teaspoons," she decided, a small indulgence she felt she deserved.

Coffee mug in hand, Esther turned to the entrance of her home, reaching into her handbag hanging on an iron hook. A momentary panic ensued as she searched for her cigarettes, but relief washed over her when her fingers brushed against the smooth surface of the nylon-wrapped pack. The elusive lighter, however, remained hidden. She rummaged through the kitchen drawer and found long, thin *Shabbat* matches. They were a resourceful alternative.

With one foot on the porch, Esther had already lit a cigarette. Her hand trembled momentarily before finding its steadiness with the first draw. She settled into one of the white garden chairs, resting her tired legs on the weathered table. The edges of her skirt cascaded down her leg, revealing freckled skin as she savored the combination of coffee and nicotine.

The phone rang inside the house, signaling the scheduled call time. Esther hesitated but decided not to abandon the second cigarette. With a deep inhale, she immersed herself in the calming habit. The phone fell silent, only to ring again after a brief pause. Esther sighed, reluctant to interrupt her moment of solitude. When the ringing stopped once again, she pulled her cell phone from her skirt pocket and dialed the familiar number, bridging the connection between her personal sanctuary and the outside world.

"Good morning, Mom," she greeted, her voice carrying a hint of a morning yawn. "Are you the one calling my landline? I couldn't answer the phone in time," she lied, trying to hide her tiredness.

"Good morning, Bushbusha Tishtasha! How are you? How are the kids? At school?" her mother inquired in the familiar cadence of their daily conversations, spoken in French as was their routine.

"Bushbusha Tishtasha" was a nickname her mom invented for her when she was a baby. She didn't know the origin or meaning behind it. Her mother, who spoke French, Arabic, and Hebrew, never revealed the reason behind the nickname. The words sounded like a made-up language, but somehow connected to her for a lifetime.

"Yes, Mom, everyone's fine. They're at school. Has Dad talked to Elie?" Esther inquired curiously.

"Why? Which Elie? And why should Dad call Elie?" A hint of confusion was present in her mother's voice as she responded.

"Elie the mover, Mom!" Esther exclaimed. She rose from her chair, planting her feet on the dew-kissed grass, and began pacing the ground in circles. A sense of urgency animated her movements.

"Why are you angry?" her mother asked, sensing the tension in Esther's voice. She felt offended by the tone. "That's not kind. I'm dealing with a lot now. It's already very challenging for me."

Esther took a deep breath, sat down, and waited in silence for the conversation to unfold. She observed the *kibbutz* landscape surrounding her, seeking its tranquility to remain calm.

"I thought you were talking about Elie, Itamar's father," her mother clarified. "Dad has already had a conversation with the mover. They set a date. I cannot remember the time they agreed on. Esther, I misunderstood your question, but it's okay to make mistakes. Even for me! Esther, am I right?"

"Right, Mom. I'm glad we're going to be neighbors in the *kibbutz*," Esther affirmed, the tension easing from her shoulders.

Mom coughed from across the line. "What are you doing today?" she asked. "Do you have any plans?"

"I don't know yet, Mom," said Esther, taking a sip of her now cool coffee.

"People often assume that individuals without a proper job are not busy," her mother remarked. "But I know what it's like to raise children. Four children—that is a lot of work. God bless them. And you, being a married woman, have a lot to take care of. You're also pursuing a master's degree at Sapir College on top of all that too! But today is not the day you're supposed to attend your class, is it? Am I right?"

"You're right, Mom. I'm going to college but only on Tuesdays," Esther replied, appreciating her mother's understanding.

"It would be great if you could come and help me pack. So, what do you say?", her mother suggested with a tentative voice.

"Come and help you pack?" asked Esther, her face buried in the collar of her sweater. It evoked childhood memories of her mother scolding her about stretching the wool.

"Only if you can," her mother assured her. "I don't want to bother you. My mom always taught me to handle things by myself, but I thought it would be nice to have you here with me."

"Of course I can come, Mom," Esther agreed. "I'm going to take a shower and will be on my way shortly." She bent over to pick up the matchbox that had dropped from her hands.

"Thank you, my daughter. I'll see you soon. I love you. You know that, right?" her mother concluded, as she often did in their conversations.

That's how she ended all her conversations with Esther. "I love you, daughter. You know that, right?" Or "I love you, daughter. Do you remember?"

Esther mumbled her reply, "Me too, Mom."

She rose from her chair and walked to her bedroom, clutching her cell phone. Lying down on the neatly made bed, she arranged the pillows under her head and stared at the white ceiling.

A few minutes later, she reached for the phone and typed, *"My mom called. I'm going to help her with the packing. It's a chance to tell her. I'll be back in the evening. Please pick up the kids. Thank you."*

Pulling a tissue from the box on the dresser, she blew her nose loudly. The cell phone beeped, and the reply read, *"Excellent. I'll take care of the kids. And take care of yourself; you know you always come back from her unsettled."*

With great effort, Esther rose and made her way to the kitchen. Filling a glass with water, she ventured out to the yard, settling on a large, rough rock. She coughed and, seeking solace, lit another cigarette. The familiar routine offered a momentary escape from the upcoming emotional conversation.

A brilliant cascade of light poured into the bathroom through the small rectangular window, illuminating every corner with a warm glow. Esther, drawn by the promise of comfort, pulled back the orange plastic curtain of the shower. She turned on the faucet and let it run until the water reached a soothing warmth.

As she sat down on the toilet lid, she couldn't shake the nagging fear that it would give way under her wide frame. Despite her apprehension, she undressed leisurely, avoiding the gaze of the mirror positioned above the compact sink.

After a refreshing shower, her hair emitted a fragrant allure, and her skin bore a reddish tint. Esther, with a thoughtful pause, opened the tap once more, grasping the bottle of liquid soap. After soaping up her arms, she scrubbed her face with a sense of purpose. She lingered at her thin mouth, the taste of soap infiltrating her senses.

Lukewarm water caressed her as she drew a line with her finger across her body, connecting to the beauty spot on her thigh. It was a ritual etched in familiarity.

Emerging from the shower, her skin radiated warmth and moisture as she wrapped herself in a towel. Moving to the sink, she brushed her teeth, then sniffed her fingers as a force of habit. The action was a subtle reminder of her youth, when she sought to mask the scent of cigarettes from her mother's discerning nose.

Finally ready to leave, Esther closed the door of the house, this time securing it with a decisive lock. The key found its place inside a gray, plastic shoe closet stationed by the door. She paused as she reached the end of the trail, retraced her steps, and double-checked the door. She needed to ease any lingering uncertainties.

On the drive to her mother's house, an uncharacteristic silence prevailed as she refrained from turning on the radio. Approaching the junction in the road, she deviated from her intended path to the right. Instead, she opted for the left turn onto the *kibbutz's* bypass road, passing the almond trees and the quiet cemetery.

Esther stopped briefly in front of a house, deep in her thoughts. She finally stepped out of the car, walked to the house, and knocked on the door with anticipation.

Nava swung the door wide open, clad in nothing but her underwear and a casual tank top. Her hair was tousled, and her eyes betrayed the remnants of a deep slumber. The unexpected sight of Nava's undressed state caught Esther off guard.

"Esther? What's going on?" Nava inquired; her voice laced with curiosity.

Esther, uncertain and taken aback, responded with a casual shrug.

"Good morning. I tried calling you, but you didn't pick up. I thought you might be upset, so I stopped by to check on you."

Nava, unfazed by the confusion, wrapped her arms around her neck and planted a kiss on the corner of Esther's lips. "What a dumb one you are," she chuckled, her laughter echoing in the room. "Come in. I'm making us coffee."

Esther was still processing the warm feeling of Nava's kiss on her skin. "I'm serious. I thought you were upset with me," she stammered.

Nava dismissed the concern with a light-hearted laugh. "Oh, you silly thing." She welcomed Esther into her cozy but disorganized home. "Let's have a coffee first, and then you can fill me in on what's happening." The door closed with a decisive thud behind them.

Esther glanced at Nava, noting the subtle contours of her body beneath the fabric of her top, where her nipples were discernible. A moment of tension lingered as Esther tried to articulate her next move. "I have to go to my mom's," she declared suddenly.

Nava, still exuding a carefree vibe, responded with a nonchalant, "Well, okay then. First things first, let's have a coffee." She moved closer to Esther, surrounding her with a certain intimacy.

Esther settled back into the car, her body glistening with a sheen of sweat. She passed through the familiar yellow gate and followed the well-worn path of Route 4, guiding her to the northern entrance of the big city. The January morning unfolded with breathtaking beauty as the sky stretched clear and wide. It reminded her of her childhood; particularly the joyous days spent with her sister Annabelle, building snowmen in the winter. The memory of her mother's involvement, giving them a carrot for the snowman's nose, remained a cherished detail from those bygone days.

Parking at the end of Lily Street, Esther found the narrow lane insufficient for her car. Crushing the dusty trail of stones beneath her feet, she made her way by walking along. A sudden bark from a dog in a nearby backyard startled her, sending shivers down her spine.

Despite the transformations that had unfolded in the Afridar neighborhood over the years, Lily Street kept its tranquil ambiance.

A nostalgic neighbor once told her, "Thirty years ago, you could see the sea from here."

While the bustling construction had altered the landscape, a hint of the once-constant sea breeze occasionally whispered through the air, carrying with it the essence of the beach.

Thinking about the changes, Esther wondered about the fate of her parents' former neighbors. How many of them were still alive? The realization struck that with each visit there were new obituaries. Once steadfast couples were now reduced to solitary figures. The house next door, once inhabited by Yaakov and Ruma, now stood as a testament to the passage of time with Yaakov living alone until his own demise.

Esther stood alone, two yards away from her parents' house. Lily Street, once a haven of companionship, now held the quiet echoes of bygone connections. It was a woven tapestry of memories and change.

The joyous laughter of a little boy echoed from a nearby courtyard. The sound created a lively backdrop as Esther stopped in front of the old wooden gate. The gate, once secured with a rusty iron chain and padlock, now featured a gleaming new golden lock. It was a strange sight to see on the dilapidated gate.

She rang the bell, and patiently awaited entry. She took in the sight of the deteriorating iron skeleton covering the parking lot and the relentless spread of rust made clear since her last visit.

As she waited, the comforting and familiar sound of her father's footsteps resonated from within the backyard. Esther's face lit up as her father, wearing square glasses and a thick beard, looked through a crack in the gate. His warm smile radiated genuine affection.

"How are you, my daughter?" With a loving gaze, he unlocked the gate.

"I'm fine, Dad. I'm here to help Mom pack," Esther replied.

Concern etched his face. Her father embraced her and asked once more, "Are you okay?"

"Yes, Dad," Esther affirmed.

"What did you say?"

"I'm fine, Dad."

"Ah, good, good," he responded with a twinkle in his eye. "Mommy's waiting for you."

His hands, weathered by time, appeared almost sculpted in a dry cast. Esther couldn't help but notice his crooked and hardened fingers, a testament to a lifetime of hard work.

"So, what are you planning? Are you only renovating the house, or is there work to be done in the yard as well?" Esther inquired.

Her father, scratching his beard, shared, "We will do what needs to be done. Who would have thought we'd be renovating a house again at our age? But this place is a daily danger. Do you see the stairs here?" He pointed towards the back door. "So dangerous, so scary. Just yesterday your mom almost fell here. It's an actual threat to her life."

He guided Esther with slow steps along the path adorned with red and blue painted pavers before revealing the tools resting in the roof's shadow—a shovel, a rake, and a road broom.

"What's going on here, Dad? Did you work in the backyard today? Was it necessary? I think it's a waste of your time. The renovation will start soon." Esther inquired, smiling at her dad.

"I grew up on a farm, remember?" her father replied, a mix of both shyness and pride clear in his tone. The memories of his childhood, once regularly exchanged with Esther, had faded over the years. He no longer opened up as he once did, erecting a silent wall between them.

The peeling, wooden back door swung open, revealing Mom standing in the doorway leading to the kitchen. Two thick red curls graced her forehead, and in the sunlight, her skin appeared thinner than ever. Speaking in French, with her hand shielding her brown eyes, she greeted Esther, "Well, why don't you come in?"

"All right, Mom," Esther replied.

"What about the kids? Everybody's okay? God bless them, Amen."

"Everyone's fine mom. No need to worry."

As Esther kissed her mother on the doorstep, the scent of sweet perfume enveloped her. Esther entered the spacious kitchen. The room appeared neat despite the crooked brown wooden cabinet doors. She noticed the flaws in both the marble table and in the red pomegranate-shaped glass bottle next to the overflowing fruit basket. The bottle was a constant reminder of a New Year's gift that her mother always mentioned.

Seating herself at the round white marble table interwoven with black veins, Esther's mother remarked, "Did you lose some weight?"

"No," Esther insisted.

"I assure you!" Her mother declared. "Esther, you don't believe me? Are you suggesting that I'm not telling the truth? You lost weight!"

Esther played nervously with the pendant of her Star of David, a childhood gift from her father.

"You must have more important things to do today. I'm bothering you with my problems. Right, Esther?" Her mother let out a sigh in frustration.

"No, Mom, of course not. Where do you want to start?"

"I don't know. We won't have time to finish everything today anyway because you arrived so late. I thought you would come right away after our phone conversation earlier today." Her mother's long fingernails scraped along the table, causing shivers to run down Esther's spine.

"Mommy, stop!" Esther exclaimed. "You're giving me chills with the noise of your fingernails."

"Sorry, sorry," her mother quickly apologized. "I didn't know it bothered you." Rising from her seat, she sighed with her back bent like an origami shape. She walked past Esther to fetch black garbage bags from the cabinet underneath the sink. "Come," she urged. "Let's start packing in my bedroom."

Her mother entered the bedroom with Esther following behind. She looked around the room with a mild expression of disgust.

"I don't like this closet," her mother declared, scrutinizing the brown wooden shelves. The clothes are always covered in dust. During the renovation, I want doors that will close. You don't have a walk-in closet, do you, Esther?"

"No, Mom. I have a regular closet."

Her mother went to the narrow shoe closet hanging on the left wall of the room. She took out pairs of butterfly-decorated stilettos and placed them on the floor. She rummaged between the predominantly black shoes and lifted one Bordeaux-colored pair in the air. "These I wore the day you arrived; the day you finally came home with us!" she declared. "I was meticulous about picking out my attire for such an important occasion. I still remember it vividly. It was such a happy day for me."

Blowing on her shoes, a small cloud of dust dispersed. "I'm impressed; these shoes are in great shape. I can't believe I've had them for so many years. Look at that buckle. Why don't you take them?"

"I'm not sure they will suit me," Esther said, examining her legs. They looked like two heavy, thick pillars. "My legs are too big."

"I haven't worn most of them in a long time either," her mother giggled. "What can I do? My legs have grown over the years."

"Just get rid of them," Esther suggested.

"It's heartbreaking to throw them away. They are very sentimental to me. At least take these," she said as she picked up a pair of pink Croc shoes with fuchsia papillon and offered them to Esther.

"I can't wear plastic." Said Esther.

Mom looked at the shoes with sadness and tossed them into a black garbage bag. "Well, out of these, I will only keep the black sneakers," she said. "You know, the flat ones that Dad bought for me. They aren't pretty, but they're comfortable. I can't walk confidently in heels like I used to when I was younger."

Esther emerged from the house with the shoe bag and placed it on the path by the gate. When she returned, she found her mother in the small walk-in closet. They both crowded inside it like two whales in a can of sardines. Esther reached out for the evening dress hanger. "Should we start with these dresses?" she asked, touching one adorned with glittering sequins. "What do you want to do with them?" Her voice carried admiration for them as she spoke.

"I thought I'd donate them," Mom replied. "I no longer have occasions to dress up for, events to attend, or reasons to go out."

"Great idea, Mom," Esther said. She took off one of the cloth corpses from its hanger and inspected it.

"I know a location for donation. I'll take them there on my way home."

Her mother emerged from the closet and stood before the bedside mirror. She sighed, placed a hand on her right hip, and scrutinized herself. Old oil stains adorned her green shirt. "Am I still pretty?" she asked. "What do you say, Esther? I'm still pretty, right? You were pretty when you were young too, remember?"

"Yes, Mom."

Esther removed dress after dress from their hangers. Among the elegant attire, a colorful floral dress emerged, seemingly younger than its counterparts.

"What is this, Mom? Is it yours?"

"This is the dress you wore on your 18th birthday. Do you remember when I bought it for you?"

"No, I don't think I do... did you really keep it? Should I put it in a 'donation' bag?"

"Oh Lord, no!!!! Put it in the moving box!"

"Really Mom, who's going to wear this?"

"It doesn't matter who wears it. It was an important day. The 18th birthday holds great significance."

A small cloth bag at the end of the shelf captured Esther's attention. She opened the bag, revealing little white balls inside, and brought it closer to her nostrils.

"Mom, are these moth balls? I can't believe you're still using moth balls to protect your closet."

"Yes, they are. I purchased them at the market. Look what happened!" she said, pointing to a mold stain that had appeared on the ceiling, kissing the base of the large golden chandelier. "Even in this room, we have leaks. It's very unpleasant."

Esther approached the rectangular window. "What about the curtains, Mom? Do you want me to take them off?"

"Yes but be careful! They're from France."

Esther carefully untangled the curtains from their hooks, folding them with care. She looked at the delicate fabric, a remnant of elegance from a bygone era. "Mom, these curtains are exquisite. We should preserve them properly."

As Esther continued her tasks, memories of the past mingled with the present. Each item held a story, a fragment of time suspended in the threads of nostalgia.

As a child, Esther would often sneak into her parents' room. She draped herself in the white curtain, pretending it was a bride's veil, lost in the innocence of her imaginative play.

"You know what, Esther?" her mother suddenly mused. "France is the most beautiful place in the world. I've been through so many homes and countries in my life. It's difficult, at my age, to move to a new place again."

Esther took a seat on the bed. "I know, Mom," she empathized. "But it's only for a few months, isn't it? The renovation will be over, and you'll be back. What would you like me to do now?"

"Here, Esther. Here on the hangers. Dad's suits. Take them off."

At her mother's request, a sweet memory blossomed in her mind: Dad in a suit, traveling by train to work during the hot summer. Her mother placed the suit in a black garbage bag.

"Well, he doesn't need the ties either," she declared. "In Israel, when can we expect him to wear them?"

In a moment, long-sleeved, buttoned-up white cotton shirts joined the ties, finding a place in the donation bag. Esther saw him one last time in her mind, envisioning her dad wearing his elegant clothes for work in 1992.

"Mom," Esther said, "Now I'm going to put the sheets here. Do you have an empty box?"

With her hands full, she said, "Esther, please be careful and put them on my bed before they fall."

Esther clasped the corner of the sheet between two fingers. "Mom, what is this fabric? Silk?" she asked.

"No, that's 100% cotton. They have been in my possession for 40 years. Your dad brought me to the Gallery Lafayette to buy them right after we got married. I hand-picked them. It was before you entered my world."

Esther observed the mound of sheets piled onto the bed: white and orange, brown and floral. Sheets in excellent condition, showcasing the best of 1970s fashion.

"Esther, I'm putting some sheets in a box for you to take home," she declared.

"I don't need them, Mom. But thank you."

"I don't want to throw them away. Hold on, Esther. I need to write what is in each box before everything gets mixed up and I forget. "

"Ok Mom," Esther said and walked away from her mother's bed.

Esther glanced at herself in the mirror adorned with flowers and fairies painted by a delicate hand. She inspected one fairy hiding among the branches and leaves, revealing a neck with a pale, round cheek resembling a doughnut. A sad look lingered in the fairy's small blue eyes.

Esther inspected her own reflection hiding amongst the branches too. What did she see in her own blue eyes? She wasn't certain at the time.

"Do you remember those flowers?" her mother asked, standing behind her and surprising her.

"Which ones?"

"The flowers!" her mother repeated, pointing to the small plastic vase underneath the mirror, holding two colorful tissue flowers. "You made me the pink flower, and your sister made the purple one, remember? You were so cute when you were little. Such good girls. That was before you started smoking and going to hang out with boys."

Esther felt irritated and fearful that she would erupt. A ringing sound echoed in the house to distract her.

"Someone's at the gate!" her mother exclaimed.

"I'm going to open it," her father declared from the other room. After a moment, they heard him speak again. "What a surprise! Mom, come and see who's here!" he cried from the kitchen.

Esther's mother emerged from the room with Esther following behind.

"Sylvie!" her mother exclaimed. Sylvie was a short-haired, thin woman with large breasts that looked like two giant balloons swelling in her tight shirt.

Her mother rushed to kiss her guest on both cheeks. "And look who else is here!" she announced. "You won't believe it. Esther's come to help me. Adorable, isn't she? She dyed her hair black again. I can't stand it. The black color makes her look tough, but she's still an adult woman, isn't she? Esther!" she continued without stopping, "Come say hello to my neighbor, Sylvie. Come on, come on, we'll have an appetizer in the living room."

Esther's father hurried to the cabinet in the living room, extracting a few bottles of liquor. From another shelf he took down the glasses that were almost never used.

"Come, Esther, sit with us," her mother urged her as she patted the couch. She turned to Sylvie. "Annabelle, my little one, couldn't make it today. She's very busy with her daughters," she said.

"I think it's best that I keep packing up in the meantime," Esther suggested. "Soon I will need to go back to my children. Why don't you sit here, and I'll start packing up the contents of the dressers?"

"God no!" her mother cried out. "I've got underpants in there. It's my underwear and your father's. I'm the only one touching those."

"Your parents, God bless them, are wonderful!" declared Sylvie half an hour later as she got up and turned to the door. "Take care of them, yes?" Esther gave her a tired smile.

"How lucky I am to have her," her mother declared after closing the door with a theatrical wave. "She takes care of me all the time. She loves me so much. Now, let me tell you a story about Sylvie and the time she took me to the mall …."

Esther's father glanced at the clock. "Do you know what time it is, darling?"

"Yes, yes," her mother said. "I'm coming to prepare lunch right away. Esther, if your dad doesn't eat at a specific time, he gets headaches," she explained on her way to the kitchen. "He wasn't like that when he was young, but he's not younger anymore and has his routine. Over the years, he became like his mother—his personality did, I mean. Come on, help me make him a salad. Did I ever tell you about that butler in Africa who worked for one of the French women there?"

"I don't recall, Mom," Esther answered, glancing at her mother.

"We were in Africa, specifically Cote d'Ivoire, because of your dad's job, and we were financially stable enough to not worry about money. Anyway, we were invited frequently to fancy dinners. It was part of the job," her mom said, standing still in the kitchen with her eyes shining.

"Yes, I remember you lived in Africa with Dad," said Esther.

"Esther, let me tell you about the time we were at a dinner, and the French ladies had butlers. We all did, but I didn't use them to cook dinner or to serve us. I used them just to do the dishes." Her mother began to laugh loudly.

"Nice," said Esther.

"Esther, are you listening? Before eating my salad, I discreetly asked one cook how he made the lettuce salad so beautiful. It looked like someone spread transparent drops of crystal on the green leaves of the lettuce—a very fancy touch, you know. He replied he put vinegar in his mouth and spat it out. Can you imagine?" Mom said as she rinsed the lettuce under the water in her kitchen sink.

"Yikes," laughed Esther.

"This is disgusting, right? There were things in Côte d'Ivoire you wouldn't be able to imagine. In four years, we saw so many weird and disgusting things. Oh my God, there were moments when it was quite frightening. Well, come on. You can wash some tomatoes for me. You're staying to have lunch with us, right?"

"Of course," Esther said. I've been here all day. What were you thinking? I'm starving." Esther unintentionally raised her voice.

"Well, well," Mom replied defensively. "What's the matter?" I asked you politely."

"Enough fighting," her father said with a strained smile. "Let's find a chair for Esther so we can all sit down and eat together."

"Not from there!" her mother cried out. "Bring a plastic chair from the backyard. I don't want the chairs to get dirty. The chairs are designer-made with a unique fabric, you know."

They sat in silence and squeezed around the small table in the kitchen.

"The lawn in my yard has grown a lot," Esther said. "Dad, would you mind giving me a hand with mowing it?"

"Of course! I'll come next week," smiled her father.

"Esther," her mother interrupted, "I have some tasks for Dad to do in our home, so you'll have to wait. He's very busy. And besides, why don't you talk after lunch? The food is getting cold."

"It's only lettuce and tomatoes," Esther pointed out. "A salad can't get cold."

Mom's face turned red. "Are you trying to make me quiet?!"

Dad's face shrunk. He slammed his fork-wielding hand on the table. "Enough is enough!" he demanded. "We're having such a lovely day together. Don't start..."

Esther got up and went out into the backyard. She sat behind the house, facing the red swing her father had set up there for the grandkids. The desire for a cigarette overwhelmed her. The yearning for the nicotine coursed through her body. Perhaps she left a pack in the car? She considered going to check, but the thought of the fight that would arise due to her absence stopped her. As she sat there, she gazed at the flowers blooming along the fence, wondering if the fragile beauty concealed a deeper truth.

After a few moments, Esther opened the door quietly and found her parents whispering by the counter in the kitchen. Together, they turned around and gazed at her.

"What you just did was wrong," Mom stated. "I'm very disappointed."

"Sorry, Mom."

"Esther, it's alright but make sure you don't repeat it, okay? He is my spouse, not yours. It's unnecessary for you to get involved when I talk to your dad."

Esther swallowed her pride and nodded. There was no point in arguing.

"Come on, Mom. Do we need to continue packing? Should we begin with the bookcase?" She pointed out the Louis XIV style cherry wood bookcase in the living room with its sealed doors at the bottom and glass showcases at the top. Her voice sounded so surprisingly childish. But whenever she stood in front of that majestic piece of furniture, it made her feel like a child. It had accompanied her parents from one house to another, even across continents. They had lived in Africa, France, Belgium—and it always seemed like a treasure chest to her.

"What's hidden inside there?" Esther asked, pointing at the bookcase's opaque bottom.

"Important things. Why are you asking?"

"I thought perhaps you wanted us to pack them in a box."

"I will do it at the end once I finish everything else."

"Mom, if you leave everything until the end, how are you going to manage the packing?"

"I completely agree with you, Esther. I apologize, but packing is incredibly overwhelming for someone my age."

"Mom, I'm here with you. We should look at what's inside first, and then you can decide." Esther smiled.

"Are you sure, Esther, do you really want us to open the bookcase?"

"Yes."

Mom giggled. "Okay, fine. Just promise me you won't touch anything! These things are both delicate and important. Esther, sometimes you behave like a young child."

Esther's mother shooed her away from the enormous piece of furniture before turning the large iron key with a green-pink wool pom-pom. As the door to the bookcase creaked open, Esther couldn't help but feel a sense of anticipation.

Each item held a chapter in her family's history, filled with memories. It was a journey through time. A glimpse into the past that held both joy and sorrow. The delicate aroma of old books wafted through the air, and Esther felt a bittersweet nostalgia enveloping her. Little did she know that within the confines of that bookcase lay not just artifacts, but the untold stories of her parents' lives.

Countless old papers became visible and filled the lower part of the bookcase. There were some unframed photographs that were counted on the side of the furniture. Mom took some of them out with a trembling hand.

"Look," she showed off a black-and-white photo from a safe distance. "It's a picture of me when I was little." She straightened up and stretched her back.

The photograph showed a little girl in an elegant white coat, standing next to a bicycle. Thick curls fell over her small shoulders. "Can you see? The cute girl in the picture is your mother at five. Look at those round cheeks. I was cute. Right, Esther?"

Esther focused on the girl's face, whose gaze was penetrating, sad, and tough. She turned her head away.

Esther approached the open furniture and carefully looked inside. Her mom was busy inspecting the vitrine on top. "Oh my God, I can't believe it!' she yelled suddenly.

"What, Esther? What are you doing? I asked you not to touch anything in there, right? What did you find?" Her mother's face lost all color as if she had just seen a ghost.

"This is mine. I recognize the logo." Esther looked at her mom with an astonished gaze. She held an envelope with "*Social Department of Children and Health*" written in large letters. Over time, certain words had vanished, except for those on the yellow envelope.

"Oh Esther, I know what you think, but I swear I'm not hiding anything from you. This is the letter you received when you were 18. You remember, right?"

"Yes, Mom, I remember," said Esther, putting the letter back into the darkness of the bookshelf.

"You know, when your dad told you that the law of France allowed you to look for your birth origin as an adult at 18, he wrote a letter for you to send to start your research after..."

"I remember, Mom," Esther interrupted. "That's all I remember. They said they couldn't help me find my origin, and that was it. What was the reason for keeping this letter for so many years?"

"I don't know Esther. It was a long time ago, and you stopped looking, so what difference does it make now?" Mom said, turning her gaze to the corner of the room. Her eyes rested upon a round wooden table displaying pictures of her children and grandchildren.

"Never mind," Esther said abruptly, rushing to the bathroom.

When Esther returned her mother pointed to a statue of a woman carved into a black tree with a small hole in her round belly.

"Esther, look at that! It's an ebony tree... very expensive wood from Africa," she proudly declared. "Living there was incredibly dangerous, you know. Even the smallest creatures like flies were dangerous. There was a high occurrence of disease. Worms that tunnel beneath the skin ... terrible. We needed to iron everything out to kill off the eggs. Then there was malaria. The medicine used to prevent it carried its own dangers. The side effects were awful, causing deafness and infertility in women. We were supposed to be in Africa for eight years, but we ended up returning to France after only four. When we arrived in Paris, I weighed only 49 kilograms, which was terrible. Once I returned to normal, your dad and I wanted to start a family since time was passing by. You know, I was getting older." Mom burst into laughter. Esther looked at her in silence.

"We did our best to get pregnant. As you already know, we discovered we couldn't. In the 70s, there weren't the treatments and options available that we have now."

Esther said nothing. She looked at the bright face of the statue resting carefully on the top shelf. She imagined an elephant's corpse next to it with its tusks sawed off.

"Have I mentioned that I once asked my sister to be a surrogate?" her mother continued. "But she's selfish. She refused, and I couldn't convince her otherwise. As I mentioned, she is selfish, unlike my daughters, who are very generous. God bless you and your sister."

"God bless you," Esther repeated.

"It all worked out for the best. I always dreamed of having a little girl with blonde hair and blue eyes, and I was blessed to get you." Mom confirmed. "You know, adopting a child requires someone with a very special character. It's the perfect act of altruism to love a child as if it were your own. And you know what, Esther? I'll tell you a secret."

She leaned over to Esther. "My approach would be even more rigid if I had a biological child, you know." Esther couldn't stop herself. She burst out laughing without restraint.

"Well, well, what is so funny, Esther?" Her mother's face reddened. We had to be vigilant because of your weak personality. Your childhood was challenging, you know."

She sighed and sank into the couch. "My legs are really swollen," she moaned, fatigue evident in her voice. "I can't stand any longer. Esther, could you go to the kitchen? There's a box of old newspapers there. Bring it, and we'll pack my mother's Tunisian mugs. You know, she received them from her grandmother. It is crucial to handle them with great care if you want to pack them. Actually, get the papers. I'll manage it on my own. If anything happens to them, I'll be devastated. On your way, do a good deed and fetch me a glass of water."

"Sure, Mom."

"Also, please ask your father to join us here and bring the ladder."

"Ok, Mom."

"I don't understand why he's retired but still spends all day on his computer. Esther, please look at the middle vitrine of the bookcase and search for the Siddur he received as a present after retiring from the *Rabbinate*. That book is a unique edition and holds significant value for your dad. I put it next to the encyclopedias. We'll pack them with the pictures of our family. I don't want it to get lost during the renovations. Oh my God, he worked there at the *Rabbinate* like a jackass. They would have killed him."

"He loved working there," Esther said. Her voice carried the weight of both nostalgia and acknowledgment.

"Love? Esther, you know nothing about what your father loves," remarked her mother. Her words were laced with a mix of bitterness and concern. "Your father suffered in that job. Every day he would come home late, and you and your sister would cry that you didn't get to see him before you went to bed."

"When we were little, Mom," Esther began, trying to bridge the gap between past and present. "But do you remember how I enjoyed going to work with him when I was a teenager? That's where I met Lehava, too. That's the place where we first crossed paths."

Her mother's expression soured at the mention of Mrs. Lehava Levy.

"Yes, I do. I remember and I can't stand her. I'd rather not talk about her. Her treatment of you was not good. She was disloyal to you."

"She wasn't, but you're right," Esther conceded, recognizing the futility of revisiting old wounds. "We shouldn't talk about it."

"She caused you a lot of trouble!" her mother continued in full swing, persistent in unraveling the threads of the past. "And who was there to get you out of the problems?! Esther, as I mentioned before, you had a weak nature. Esther, what is going on? Where are you going?"

"I'll return shortly," Esther declared, resolute, already positioned by the door. Maybe she'd find a cigarette in her car after all.

∽

When Esther finally returned, she yelled down the corridor connecting the living room to the other rooms. "Dad, do you want to join us and sit together?"

Mom, still occupying the couch, lifted her feet off the small table and sighed. "We've had enough time to sit down," she said. "Let's get back to packing. It's important that we finish packing everything before the renovation starts."

"Just a moment, please," Esther insisted.

"Where have you been, by the way?" You know we have lots to pack."

Her father took a slow step from his study and settled into his regular armchair.

"Did you bring the ladder?" Mom asked.

"I am pretty sure Esther has something to tell us." he responded while looking at Esther.

They both stared at her, anticipating the imminent revelation.

"I do have something to tell you," Esther said, her words carrying a gravity that echoed through the room. "Itamar has decided we are going to France."

"That's what you came for? To ask us to look after the kids?" her mother asked, a mix of surprise and willingness in her tone.

"We will be glad to help, Esther," her father offered, turning his head to his wife. "Let her speak," he ordered, sensing there was more to unfold.

"Well, fine. I'd love to," Esther's mother said with both curiosity and caution.

"No," said Esther, her voice steadying. "I mean, yes. But that's not what I wanted to share with you. We're going to look for my mother … my birth mother."

The room fell into an awkward silence, absorbing the weight of Esther's revelation and the unspoken complexities that lay ahead.

Chapter 2

Lehava

Paris, France | July 1992

*E*sther's father came home from work late, as usual. The day wore on his shoulders, and each step he took from the train station echoed a quiet weariness.

A brown leather bag swung by his side. His left hand navigated through the pockets of his suit, one among the many he had worn throughout the year.

The black iron gate, adorned with golden balls, stood as a sentinel amid the row of small houses, their pink façades glowing in the fading light.

Upon entering the house, he shed the gray hat and the suit jacket, symbolic of the role he played every day. The jacket found its place on the wooden sling at the foot of the stairs, topped by the hat. He loosened his deep marine blue tie with a sigh of relief. He was happy to change into more comfortable clothing suited for the warm weather.

At dinner time they all shared a little about their day. The girls discussed school, with a focus on homework and grades. Dad always had a fun story to share, typically about someone from the community seeking his help. Mom talked about staying at home, doing laundry, or running errands. "Nothing exciting here," she would always say at the end of dinner. It was always this way with the four of them.

The atmosphere shifted as Annabelle, their younger daughter, announced her need for the bathroom. She retreated to the first-story sanctuary for her usual prolonged visits.

Esther, the eldest daughter, stood up to clear the leftovers from the table. Most of the time, it was chicken and rice. Chicken was more affordable, even at the kosher butchery. Since they came back from Israel a few years ago, their budget was tight. They had lost a lot of money in Israel. Dad's paycheck went towards the mortgage of the house they had bought. Dad wasn't ready to spend so much money on rent.

"Hold on a moment, Esther. I need to talk to you," he said, capturing Esther's attention. A certain seriousness lingered in his gaze as he poured water into his glass.

After putting down the plates, Esther returned to her seat. Her father asked, "Do you want to go with me to the office tomorrow?"

Esther's eyes widened in surprise, and a burst of excitement prompted her to dance on the padded chair. "Really?"

"I could use a hand. The election is approaching soon," her father explained.

"I'm not sure which election you're talking about."

"Of the *Rabbinate,* Esther," he clarified. "The summer break is starting, and I don't think you have any plans."

Esther smiled, her excitement growing.

"What happened? Where is she going with you?!" Mom interrupted, emerging from the kitchen.

Dad raised his hand to signal her to stop talking. Her face flushed with concern as she fell silent, settling into her chair with an air of tension. She scraped her long fingernails across the yellow tablecloth to show her agitation.

"I don't understand why there's a problem, darling," Esther's father told his wife. He was only expressing his desire for their daughter to go with him to work.

After a brief pause, he redirected his attention to Esther. "I'll wake you up tomorrow morning at 6:00 am."

Esther glanced down at the table. "So early?"

"Indeed, so early," her father confirmed. "We've talked enough. Now, let's clean the table." The prospect of a new adventure and shared responsibilities cast a different light on the mundane task of table cleaning.

"Good morning, Esther! It's time to get up!" said Dad as he opened the shutters.

Esther opened her eyes. A few days earlier she had sat on the windowsill overlooking the backyard where she worked with Dad every Sunday. Her legs were shaking in the air above the white rosebush, the blueberries, and raspberries. Beneath it, only the gentle grass and the beloved scent of the land with no safety net in sight. She had wanted to spread her arms to fly but knew she would crash to the ground and explode like an overripe watermelon.

She came back from her reverie and closed her eyes once again.

"The train we need to take will arrive soon, and you still need to get ready. Hurry please," her father urged her. "I can't be late to work. Please keep it quiet. Don't wake Annabelle."

Esther got out of bed slowly and started getting dressed. She opted for a shiny gray skirt with a wide black rubber belt, topped off with an elegant bottle-green button-up shirt. She was going to the *Rabbinate,* after all.

When she went down to the first floor, her black heeled shoes were waiting for her to put on. Her gaze fell upon the breakfast table, where the remnants of her father's breakfast remained. It was always the same: black coffee, a remedy for his headaches, and two slices of bread with butter and jam. It had been his regular breakfast since he was a child.

"I'm ready," she stated in a weary voice as she walked out of the dining room. She leaned against the wall by the front door and lowered her arms beside her body.

"Esther, are you sure you don't want to eat? Breakfast is the most important meal of the day."

Esther shook her head, graciously declining the offer. "No, it's okay. I'll grab a coffee later."

At the door, her father put on his gray hat over a black crocheted *kippah,* signaling the start of their day's journey.

Wandering beyond Capselles Alley, Dad and Esther took a right onto Bastin Street, immediately followed by a left onto General de Gaulle Boulevard. The iron shutters of the shops lining the boulevard remained closed, preserving the quietness of the early morning.

"Look, all the shops are still closed. Only the bar is open," Esther observed. "What could they possibly be doing there so early?"

A chuckle escaped her father's lips. "I see them every morning. They are drinking red wine as early as 6:00 am. Real Frenchmen."

Esther yawned. "Disgusting!" she proclaimed.

'*Sarcelles Saint Brice*'

The white letters on the blue, rectangular ceramic sign were proudly displayed above the entrance of an unassuming building at the boulevard's end. To the casual observer, the structure might have seemed like a regular home. It was crafted from sizable gray stones and crowned with a red tile roof. Dark glass windows adorned with iron bars added an air of mystery to it.

Dad held the door open for Esther. Despite the early hour, a bustling crowd had already gathered inside. Most stood, with only a fortunate few claiming the sole wooden bench.

"I'll get you a ticket; wait for me here," her father instructed.

Esther nodded, momentarily caught in a daydream. She pictured women in voluminous dresses, gracefully circling the center of the spacious room. They bathed in the glow of an opulent chandelier. Imaginary men, adorned in elaborate white wigs, scrutinized their every move with discerning gazes.

"Here, Esther." Her father interrupted the scene playing in her mind. He handed her an orange, rectangular card with a bold black line. "Keep it safe. You'll need it to exit the Paris station."

Casting a glance at the sizable analog clock above the station door, her father urged, "Come on. The train should arrive in two minutes." The air buzzed with commuters and travelers readying themselves for the day's adventures. The station bore witness to the daily ebb and flow of bustling life.

"Attention, please. The train for Paris is entering the station. Stay behind the white line until the train stops," said a speaker above their heads.

Dad and Esther watched as a tin-colored train came to a stop on platform number one. Hurriedly, they climbed the stairs and found a wagon already filled with smoke from white cigarettes. Esther's father, coughing from the fumes, motioned for her to follow him to the next carriage. The satisfying hiss of air escaping from the train car door brought a subtle smile to Esther's lips.

They kept walking through the train car, searching for room to sit. Finally, they found two vacant seats.

With each passing station, the train filled up with more passengers. As the capital grew nearer, only a few disembarked.

The train's rhythmic sway made Esther feel sleepy.

"Mademoiselle? Ticket please," a gentleman said gently, attempting to rouse her from her daze.

Shaking off the encroaching slumber, Esther handed him her ticket. "Merci, Monsieur," she acknowledged.

"Merci, Mademoiselle," replied the man, tipping his hat courteously.

Esther smiled, diverting her gaze to the passing landscape. Low houses, colorful tiled roofs, and towering trees painted a familiar picture. It was reminiscent of her childhood home.

As the train approached the next station, a sign came into view: '*Montmagny.*'

Esther turned to her father. "Dad, this is where Grandma lives, right?"

He nodded in agreement, and Esther's smile widened. Her father had often regaled she and her sister with tales of his youth in a French village. He recounted many escapades he and his younger brother had shared.

"When I was young, my brother and I were always on adventures. We're close in age, with him being just one year younger than me. I remember one day we were chasing cats. When we finally caught the poor animals, we grabbed them by the tail and spun them around, sending them flying into the air. Luckily, cats have nine lives. We were so young; I don't know how we survived." Dad smiled.

"Oh my God, that reminds me of when we worked in the backyard for the first time a few days after we moved in. We found so many strange objects when we dug. I remember we pretended to be pirates, looking for treasures to pass the time." Esther had a huge grin on her face.

"You know, Esther," her dad continued, "When we were in elementary school, we would milk a cow before school and make cheese when we were back home."

"Dad, that's crazy," Esther said.

"Ladies and gentlemen, welcome to *La Gare du Nord*, our last stop," announced a male voice over the train's intercom. The expansive central station unfolded before Esther's eyes. The powerful scent of motor oil and smoke created a rich atmosphere.

Dad made deliberate steps towards the bustling bus terminal. Esther followed closely behind. The journey involved a lengthy bus ride followed by a brisk walk. It culminated with their arrival at 15 Saint George Street in the 9th *arrondissement* of Paris. It was home to the imposing Main *Rabbinate* Building. Esther marveled at its stature, observing its seamless integration with its urban surroundings.

As they reached the entrance, Esther stood before a massive green wooden door etched with intricate details. A security camera silently watched them.

While they waited for the guard to unlock the door, Esther diverted her attention to the sidewalk. The ground was marred by pigeon excrement, creating an unexpected palette of colors.

A distinctive beep sounded through the air as her father forcefully pulled the heavy door, granting them access to the hidden inner courtyard.

"Good morning," her father warmly greeted the guard behind a transparent separation wall. "This is my daughter,

Esther. She's here to assist us today." With a slight gesture, he encouraged Esther to offer her salutation.

"Good morning," she echoed, unable to tear her gaze away from the deep trenches etched into the guard's weathered face.

Beyond the guard post, a spacious waiting area sprawled before them, filled by a diverse group of people. Some wore smiles that spoke of shared camaraderie, while others bore expressions of sorrow, hinting at the complex tapestry of emotions that defined this communal space.

"The administration placed the *Chevra Kadisha* and the wedding department side by side," her father whispered to her. "Every morning it's like this. People are crying and people are laughing. It's a surreal experience."

He swung open another door, and a wave of musty odor engulfed them. Esther's attention turned to a metal cage resembling a mechanical structure.

"Is that the elevator?" she inquired.

"Yes," her father replied. "But we're taking the stairs. It's faster."

Ascending a set of long, winding wooden stairs, they entered a dimly lit, yellow stairwell. Reaching the upper floor, her father pulled a key from his pocket and unlocked a large, Bordeaux-colored wooden door. Behind it, a silence shrouded in darkness seemed to have lingered overnight. Dad fumbled along the wall, searching for the switch. The light flickered momentarily before illuminating the room allowing Esther to breathe again. She hated the dark.

"Where is everybody?" asked Esther.

"My employees will be here soon. As the head of the department," he said with pride, "I need to be the first one here."

Guiding her through the corridor, Dad sequentially flipped the light switches. When he reached his office, he sighed and removed his gray hat, reaching up to adjust his *kippah*. His thin hair was adorned with white dandruff flakes.

An hour and a half had elapsed since they left the house. Esther kicked off her shoes, feeling the cool floor beneath her feet. The faint voices from the corridor suggested employees were coming.

Esther's father stood up and went to the door.

"Lehava Levy, good morning!" he called out. "Come into my office, please!"

A wide-bodied, curly-haired woman entered the room, her face powdered white with makeup.

"What is it, Monsieur Elbaz?"

"Lehava, I'd like to introduce you to my daughter, Esther."

Lehava burst into laughter. "You gave me such a fright. I thought I was in trouble," she said in Hebrew. A mischievous smile spread across Esther's father's face.

Esther scrutinized Lehava, taking in her unexpected ensemble of jeans paired with a crisp white T-shirt. As her eyes lingered, a perplexing thought crossed Esther's mind: '*Where on earth did Lehava find those glasses?*' It was as if she had stumbled upon them in a Kinder Egg surprise.

"Esther, I'd like to introduce you to Lehava Levy. She recently joined our office after moving from Israel with her spouse and children. She's still learning French, but she catches on quickly. You mentioned missing someone to speak Hebrew with, so …" Esther's father glanced at his watch while talking to them.

Lehava smiled and reached out her hand to Esther.

Before Lehava could say anything, Esther greeted her in Hebrew with a "Nice to meet you."

"Wow, you already know Hebrew!" Lehava exclaimed. "Where'd you learn that?"

"When Esther was little, we lived in Israel for a few years, in a *Moshav* near Jerusalem," Esther's father explained. "Alright, let's get to work. But now that you guys know each other, I'm sure you'll have tons to talk about, in both Hebrew and French!" he added cheerfully.

"Let's grab lunch together at noon. I know a cool restaurant already. What do you think, Esther?" Asked Lehava.

"Absolutely!" Esther proudly replied in Hebrew.

Esther's father opened the door. "Good morning!" he announced to the employees. "May I have your attention for a moment?"

Silence draped over the office. The employees, arranged in a long, narrow column table by table, looked up at him.

"Mademoiselle Cohen, are you coming?" he called to his secretary in the adjacent office.

After capturing the employees' attention, he signaled Esther and Lehava to leave his office.

"Allow me to introduce my daughter, Esther," he announced. "She's here to assist us today. Esther, say good morning please!"

"Good morning," Esther greeted in a small voice.

❧

At 11:50 AM, Lehava stood in front of Esther's desk, positioned at the end of the hall.

"Esther, are you coming to eat?" Lehava inquired.

Esther turned her head, relieving her stiff neck. "Sure," she replied. "I'll just confirm with my dad, alright?"

"100 percent," assured Lehava. "I'm going to grab my purse. We'll meet next to the elevator." She said.

Esther knocked on her father's office door and entered without waiting for a response. A white napkin adorned his desk, accompanied by two sandwiches and a green apple.

"Esther!" he exclaimed. "Will you be joining me for lunch?"

"I planned to go out and have lunch with Mrs. Levy," Esther replied.

"Great," her father said. He retrieved a small notepad from the drawer and tore out some colorful tickets. "Esther, take those. Use them to cover the cost of your lunch. All the restaurants in the area take them. Bon appétit."

Lehava was already waiting at the elevator. "Esther are you ready?" she asked in Hebrew. "The lunch break only lasts for one hour."

Hundreds of workers spilled out of the towering office buildings precisely at twelve o'clock. They streamed into the nearby restaurants with a sense of urgency. They behaved like robots donned in impeccably tailored suits. Lehava and

Esther, amidst the bustling crowd, made a right turn onto St. George Street.

"I've already discovered an amazing spot here," Lehava mentioned. "Do you like falafel? It's an Israeli place." Esther followed her closely. She marched on from sidewalk to sidewalk, and street to street, passing boulevards, no-entry signs, and hurried cars.

The moment they stepped into the restaurant, Lehava's face lit up and a wide smile appeared. "Hi! What's going on?" she exclaimed aloud. She turned to Esther. "He's the owner. Please, have a seat. I'll order. Do you like falafel? Do you like spicy food?"

Esther sat down in the restaurant's corner. She had doubts about whether she liked falafel and was hesitant about the spiciness. She hadn't had Israeli food since she was eight. Lehava came back with a loaded tray. "Would you like something to drink?" she asked.

"Yes, thank you, I would love a Coke," Esther replied. She showed the ticket she had received from her father.

"Lehava, I have to pay."

Lehava laughed. "Today, I am treating you to lunch," she proclaimed. "God bless you," she added in Hebrew.

The hunger Esther felt was so intense, she thought she was dying.

"Well, tell me about yourself," Lehava said. "How old are you?"

"Seventeen and a half," Esther replied with her mouth full, raising a hand to hide the crushed food falling from her mouth as she talked. "I'm almost eighteen, actually."

"Do you still go to school?" Lehava asked between bites.
"Yes."

"By the time I reached your age, I had already completed my first army order and became part of the army in Israel. What a good time! Is military service not mandatory here?"

"No."

"Never mind," laughed Lehava. "Do you want some tahini? It's good for your health."

Without waiting for an answer, she reached out and squeezed the sauce from the plastic bottle onto Esther's plate.

"Thank you," said Esther. "I understand that you have children. How old are they?"

"I have three boys. God bless them. Inbar is eight years old, Idan is six years old, and Einav is three years old. I'm totally obsessed with them."

"So nice! I want a bunch of kids, too. I only have one sister, and it's boring. She's very young, so there's nothing to chat about with her."

"If you're all about kids," Lehava said, "perhaps you'd be up for babysitting my kids? They're so adorable. And I'll pay you, for sure. What do you think?"

"I'd love to, but I need to ask my parents for permission first."

"Great," smiled Lehava. "My husband and I desperately need some free time," she glanced at her watch and quickly got up. "O-la-la! Check out the time. Your Dad is going to murder me."

∽

"You've been productive today," Esther's father remarked as they rode the elevator down after work. "Well done. You can come work in the office with me all summer."

Esther let out a shout of joy. Her father giggled.

∽

Lehava glanced up from her cluttered desk, her eyes meeting Esther's as she spoke. "I hope you remember that you're coming to my house to babysit tonight."

Esther, on her way from the bathroom, responded with a simple, "Sure."

"Good," Lehava continued. "Why are you working there in the corner?"

Esther blushed and confessed, "It's too quiet for me over there. No one passes by because it's at the end."

With a gesture of hospitality, Lehava suggested, "Why don't you move into my office? There's a desk I'm not using here. Honestly, it's boring being alone here."

Considering the offer, Esther replied, "I'll check with my dad first." She left the room and went to her father's office, disrupting his work. "Can I join Lehava in her office? It's packed in the corridor."

"Do you really think that's a good idea?" Dad asked, lifting his head.

"Yep," she said.

"Alright. You understand you need to keep working, right? Seriously, no talking. Is it possible for you to make it work?"

"Yes, of course." Esther said confidently.

"Okay, fine. Don't forget to turn off the computer."

Returning to her desk, Esther saved the open file on the screen and powered down the computer. With the screen dimmed, she straightened the chair beside the table and made her way to Lehava's office. She smiled as she went, ready for a change of scenery.

"How fun!" Lehava declared with enthusiasm, rising from her chair to greet Esther. "I'm bored here! Here, the desk next to mine is vacant. You can sit down. Do you need help to turn on the computer?"

"No, I'm fine," Esther responded as she settled into the chair. Leaning back, she felt the dampness of sweat on the back of her shirt.

Lehava, standing up, reached behind her back. A moment later, her slender bra straps emerged from the short sleeves of her shirt, and she casually tossed the bra into her bag. "I can't stand it anymore!" she declared. "That bra was killing me. Look, wait, can you see anything?" Turning to Esther, she pointed to her breasts, and Esther burst into laughter.

"You're crazy," Esther remarked.

"Well, look!"

"I can't see anything."

"Good," said Lehava. "Now do it, too! Take off your bra. And don't make any noise because your father will fire me." Esther shook her head no emphatically.

"What are you afraid of?" laughed Lehava. "Your breasts are so tiny. What are you worried about?" Esther glanced toward her father's office. She hesitated before reaching for the clasps of her bra.

"Do you need anything?" Esther heard a voice call as she looked out the door. At the entrance to the office stood Mr. Abitbol, one of the oldest employees there.

Lehava giggled. "What do YOU need, Monsieur Abitbol?" she asked.

His face blushed. "I thought you needed help because I heard a loud noise coming from here," he explained.

"No, we were just laughing," Lehava said, looking at him with round eyes.

"Esther, do you need anything?" asked Monsieur Abitbol, who was standing at the door quietly.

"No, thank you, I'm fine. We're okay. Sorry about the noise." Replied Esther.

"He looks like an old baboon," giggled Lehava, as Monsieur Abitbol walked past the large glass window of her office. "Look at the way he looks at us. We're like sea monsters in an aquarium. Maybe he wants to feed us?"

"Did you take your pajamas? A towel? Your toothbrush?" Dad asked Esther with concern in his voice.

Already dressed in her pink jacket and ready to leave, Lehava comforted Monsieur Elbaz. "No need to worry. If she needs anything, I'll give her my own."

"Don't worry, Dad," Esther said, attempting to hide her excitement in his presence. It was the first time she would not be going home with Dad. It was her first time sleeping in a stranger's house. "See you tomorrow morning. I'll come to work with Lehava."

"Tomorrow morning, be here at the office at 8:00 am sharp. Don't be late," her father reminded her. "Please call your mother as soon as you arrive at Lehava's house this evening."

Esther and Lehava chose the old stairs, quickly passing by the elevator. "To reach the metro station, we'll need to walk for about 15 minutes," Lehava cautioned. "I hope you're okay with walking."

"I love walking," Esther replied. She smiled joyfully, bouncing down the street with renewed energy.

"We need line number eight for Créteil. This is one of the longest lines on the RER, with many stops along the way." Lehava said as they reached the underground station.

"I've never been to Creteil," Esther said.

"Soon you'll see that it was worth coming," Lehava said. "Israel prepares Israeli food. He excels in the kitchen."

The metro line rumbled beneath the ground like an iron snake. Above them, Esther saw the signs for all the stops along their train's route:

Richelieu-Drouot, Grands Boulevards, Bonne
Nouvelle, Strasbourg-Saint-Denis, République,
Filles du Calvaire, Saint-Sebastien-Froissart,
Chemin Vert, Bastille, Ledru-Rollin, Faidherbe-
Chaligny, Reuilly-Diderot, Montgallet, Daumesnil,
Michel Bizot, Porte Dorée, Porte de Charenton,
Liberté, Charenton-Écoles, Marne, École
Vétérinaire de Maisons-Alfort, Maisons-Alfort-
Stade, Maisons-Alfort-Les Juilliottes, Créteil-
L'Échat, Créteil-Université

"Créteil–Préfecture!" declared Lehava. "This is the station where we get off. Come on, Esther!"

As they left the station, the high streetlights flickered into existence, illuminating their path to Lehava's house as the train carried on to its last stop.

"We only have a couple more minutes of walking left. Don't worry." Said Lehava. Esther didn't reply.

As Lehava opened the door of her ninth-floor apartment, her husband and three children were already waiting in the doorway. Israel, a tall man with hints of gray in his short hair, greeted Esther with a firm handshake. "Very nice to meet you. I am Israel," he said.

Lehava immediately asked, "Israel, have the kids eaten dinner yet?"

"They just finished."

Lehava casually dropped her purse on one chair and sank into the inviting black sofa. "Esther, come sit with me," she called out. Esther took a few steps into the apartment, examining her surroundings with keen interest. The atmosphere was warm and inviting, and Esther felt a sense of comfort settling in.

There was a closed door on the left, next to where the kitchen opened. On the right stood a large dining table made of glass, its legs black and surrounded by six black chairs. "Sit down, come on," said Lehava. Esther sat down on one of the black armchairs. Feeling slightly out of place, as she looked awkwardly at the sleek black table. "I've had enough of these heels," Lehava exclaimed, discarding her shoes. Her little boy quickly settled on her lap. "It's almost bedtime, and then we'll be out," Lehava told Esther. "In the meantime, I'll show you around the apartment."

During Lehava's guided tour, they passed the corridor, toilet, shower, and the neatly arranged children's rooms.

"Come to my bedroom. I need to get ready," Lehava said, leading Esther to a room where a double bed dominated most of the space. Lehava approached the closet, tucked into the corner of the room, and pulled out a stylish skirt and a sleek black shirt. She placed her clothes on the bed and looked herself over in the mirror. "I have to wear makeup," she declared. "Oh, my goodness, I look terrible!"

Esther sat down on the edge of the bed, taking in the unfamiliarity of being in someone else's bedroom. The room exuded a mix of personal touches and functionality. Jewelry, makeup, creams, and perfumes were all neatly arranged on the small dresser underneath the rectangular mirror.

Lehava opened one of the blush boxes, turned to Esther, and dabbed two pink puffs on Esther's cheeks. "You can also try the perfume," she suggested.

Opening the perfume bottle, she brought it close to Esther's nose. "Try it, it's fantastic. I'm going to say good night to the kids."

As Lehava left the room, Esther hesitated for a moment, then experimented with the perfume. She immersed herself in the unfamiliar scents that filled Lehava's personal space.

That night, Lehava and her husband returned home after enjoying dinner at a fancy restaurant. They lay in bed, sharing laughter and joy.

Meanwhile, Esther reclined on a mattress in the dimly lit living room.

Suddenly, the laughter ceased, and in the night's stillness, Esther heard unusual noises coming from Lehava. Unsure whether Israel was causing her distress or if everything was alright, Esther struggled to understand what was happening.

Following one more peculiar and loud sound, tranquility returned to the darkened household.

"Lehava asked me to join her family for a *Shabbat*. Can I?" Esther asked her mother.

"Are you going to her house again?" her mother raged. "It's already the fifth time this month. Maybe that's enough? How much babysitting does this woman need? Why don't you just do a Sabbath here with us instead of outside the house, so you don't leave your sister like this alone?"

"She invited me to an Israeli breakfast on Saturday morning," Esther explained. I told her I couldn't travel on Saturday because of *Shabbat,* which is why she suggested I come on Friday night."

"When can we expect you to come back home?" Mom and Dad asked with one voice.

"Monday morning, straight to Dad's office. We'll be riding the metro together. Anyway, you won't let me go alone."

"Why are you going for so long, Esther? You can come home on Saturday night," her mother insisted.

"She wants to take me to the Creteil Soleil Mall. It's a huge mall, and I …"

"I want to go to the mall too!" declared Annabelle. She met her father's brown eyes ("Almond eyes," as their mother called them). "Can I?" her little sister asked.

"We can't afford to shop for unnecessary things," her mother stated.

"I didn't ask for money," Esther replied. Her forehead folded like an accordion. "I wanted to go check out the stores. Plus, it's fun for me to chat in Hebrew with Lehava and her family. It's always good to know another language, right? That's what you always say."

Esther's parents exchanged glances, and her father sighed. "Okay, okay. Take care of yourself, and don't make it a habit, alright?"

∽

"Esther, come on," Lehava urged on a quiet Sunday afternoon. Israel had taken the children to the park, leaving the house in a peaceful hush. Earlier that morning, Israel had prepared a delightful Israeli breakfast. It featured eggs, *Bourekas* and a vibrant salad cut into small, colorful pieces. The freshness of lemon and olive oil added a delightful touch to the meal.

"I have something to teach you." She put her coffee cup on the table and headed towards the bathroom. Esther got up and followed her to the small room, covered in greenish ceramics. "Come in. Why are you standing at the door like that?"

"I thought you wanted to take a shower," Esther said.

"I'm fine. You're the one taking a shower."

"What, now?" Esther asked, surprised.

"Yes, you are. Come on, I want to show you something."

Intrigued, Esther hesitated, but eventually complied, stepping into the bathroom. Little did she know that this impromptu moment would lead to an unexpected lesson and a bond between the two of them.

"I know how to shower," laughed Esther.

Lehava nodded. She opened the water tap. A strong current of water burst from the top of the shower head.

Lehava put her hand under the flowing water. "Good, it's warm," she said. "So come on, I'm going out and you are … come on."

"Come on, what?" Esther asked, surprised and unsure.

"Come on, you get in the shower and play," Lehava said. She directed her gaze between Esther's legs. Esther became paralyzed. "Well, what do you want, a drawing?" said Lehava.

"What?" asked Esther.

"Well, come on, Esther, are you serious?! You are so naive." asked Lehava.

"Put the water stream down there and play. It's fun, you'll see. You're really stressing me out. Oh my God! You're old enough now. It's time to learn about your G-spot."

Esther swallowed hard.

Lehava smiled. "What are you worried about? Everything's going to be ok, don't worry!"

"I never … you know," Esther whispered, looking down at the floor.

"It's ok. Just don't make too much noise. Israel could come back with the kids at any moment, and it would be awkward, you know." She winked and closed the door behind her.

Esther went over and locked the door. Removing her shirt and peeling off her socks and jeans, she examined her reflection in the mirror above the sink. She removed her bra and underwear and stepped into the shower, laying down on the cool ceramic. She then spread her legs, reached up for the showerhead, and turned the current on her body. Her eyes closed and with her other hand, she opened her pubic lips. Her wet body shuddered, and a small voice broke out of her throat. She put her hand over her mouth to stifle the noise.

Esther, dressed in jeans and a white T-shirt, huddled with the three children in the backseat of a white Ford. After a long drive, Israel parked on a narrow street in the Sentier neighborhood of central Paris. Esther had never visited the neighborhood, known for its wholesale clothing stores. On Sunday it was almost completely deserted.

She looked around at the tall buildings whose windows were so wide. Colorful signs proclaiming business names stood like dense dominoes one by one. A miniature *Arc de Triomphe* stood at the end of the street. Israel locked the car, and they entered the centuries old Parisian building.

"What kind of business did they open here?" Esther whispered to Lehava as they walked up a creaking wooden staircase.

"Some weird business, don't ask," she shrugged.

Israel opened a black wooden door. "Hi!" he exclaimed from the doorway. "Hi!" a voice replied from inside.

Dusty plastic-wrapped rolls of cloth were stacked on the parquet floor. A solid, small man crossed the void between them and came to greet them.

"So, Samuel, you have a front desk, but you don't have a receptionist?" laughed Israel. His big teeth stood out.

A young man with black hair emerged from one of the side doors.

"Almog!" Lehava squealed. "Come, Esther, let me introduce you to Almog, my nephew. Almog, this is Esther. She wanted to meet Israelis, so I started teaching her Hebrew."

The room was electric when Esther met Almog.

The makeshift office exuded an artistic charm, with its rolls of richly colored fabrics. Esther wondered what sort of tales these walls might tell if they could speak.

As Almog warmly greeted her, Esther sensed a connection that transcended cultural boundaries. Little did she know that this unexpected encounter would become another woven layer in the tapestry of her Parisian adventure.

Almog reached out his hand to Esther. "Very nice to meet you," whispered Esther. His fingers were hard and warm.

The black wooden door opened, swinging behind them. Esther turned around. A bald, short man in a brown leather jacket and faded jeans bustled in like a storm wind.

"Almog!" he shouted. You will not believe what happened to me!

His hands and feet moved haphazardly as he spoke, as if he were a puppet on wires. His long eyelashes went up and down like a fan. Esther had trouble taking her eyes off him. She examined the bristles on his face. She slowly surveyed his body all the way to the light blue All-Star shoes at his feet. He looked back at her.

"Nice to meet you. I am Amir," he said as he approached and shook her hand.

"In France, you give four kisses when you meet," said Esther struggling to speak in Hebrew. She blushed knowing it wasn't coming out quite right. "You're from Israel, right? I love Israel. I lived there from kindergarten to second grade."

"You don't like France?" asked Almog.

"It's fine, but I still miss Israel," Esther replied.

"Well, maybe one day you'll go back," Almog said in Hebrew. "You never know."

Amir turned to Almog and began speaking with a fluency in Hebrew that Esther could not follow. The smell of his cologne was spicy and sweet. She inhaled it deeply into her nostrils.

The room seemed to come alive with the vibrant exchange of languages, each word carrying a piece of a diverse cultural tapestry. Esther felt a mixture of excitement and curiosity as she continued her unexpected encounter with Amir. His animated gestures and expressive demeanor were charged with energy. She had no idea this intersection of cultures would open a new chapter in her journey. It would reveal the intricate threads connecting her to the vibrant Israeli community in the heart of Paris.

"Amir and Almog invited me to go to a club with them!" Esther pounced on Lehava as she returned from her tour of the business. "What do you say? Can I go with them? Please-please?"

Lehava laughed. "Yes, sure, enjoy yourself. Here, I'll give you money."

She took out a 500 Francs bill and a piece of paper from her purse, wrote her address, and handed it to Amir.

"Here's my address in Créteil," she said. "She'll stay at my place tonight, so bring her there, okay? Thanks, love." She looked at Esther. "Your dad's going to murder me," she laughed again. "He gave me this innocent girl and look at what I've turned you into."

"I won't tell my dad, so don't worry, okay?" Esther spoke in a serious tone.

Lehava instructed the three teenagers, "Okay, enjoy yourselves. Don't stay out too late." She smiled as they departed.

Amir opened the front door of the white Citroën Berlingo waiting for them in the parking lot.

"You have a car?" Esther asked, clearly impressed.

"This is our business vehicle," Amir stated. He sat behind the wheel and pulled a cassette out of his pocket. The music played from the speakers as he started the car.

"Who's the singer?" asked Esther.

"Avi Bitter," said Amir, patting the steering wheel to the beat. "Do you like it?"

"Yes," said Esther.

During the long drive, she looked out the window and periodically glanced at Amir as he drove with one hand. They finally parked in front of a wide, single-story building. The place was remote and away from any residential buildings. Its surroundings were almost completely dark, like an abandoned field.

"Do you have an ID?" asked Almog as they got out of the car.

"Yes," said Esther with a sense of satisfaction.

As they entered, she removed the card from her pocket. She bounced up and down. She felt an abrupt transformation as she matured. Almog looked at her and giggled. She smiled at him and kept jumping.

"Cheers!" declared Almog, waving his beer bottle in the air.

Esther brought the bottle to her mouth and sipped. "Disgusting," she whispered to herself.

"*Drinking alcohol is not good for your health.*" she recalled her mother saying more than once. "*It's harmful. It can consume the liver.*"

She sipped again, and her mom's voice dissipated.

After a few moments, all three of them rose from the bar with bottles in their hands. They moved from one space to another as if they were visiting a museum. Esther's head was spinning.

"Come on, there's snooker here!" cried Amir.

"And pinball," Almog noted.

One of the other spaces had loud music playing. Esther moved her body from side to side. "I love dancing," she smiled at Amir as he watched her.

"We don't dance," he said.

❧

"Good night, Esther," Amir said as they stopped in front of Lehava's building in Créteil. The ride back had passed quickly. The roads were almost empty, and Amir didn't always stop at red lights.

"Good night, thank you very much!"

She paused for a moment before getting out of the car, hoping Amir would kiss her. He sat drumming on the steering wheel.

She got out, slamming the white car door behind her and ran into the building. The rhythm of the night echoed in her ears. The echoes of laughter and music intertwined with the thrill of newfound freedom.

As she climbed the stairs, Esther couldn't shake the sense that this night had marked a turning point for her. It marked a departure from the familiar into a world pulsating with life and exhilaration.

❧

"Esther! What a surprise! Are you back working with us? asked Lehava.

Several weeks had passed since their last meeting during the summer holidays, and they had not seen each other since. Esther told her she didn't have school today and asked her dad if she could visit.

"Why don't you come and help me for a minute? Sit down, sit down ... I need you to file some papers," said

Lehava, pointing to a tall pile of rectangular pages on the table. "You need to file them into the binders behind you, okay? By alphabetical order."

"No problem," Esther said. She touched her neck, fiddling with the Star of David on the gold necklace her dad had given her on her eighteenth birthday. "Hey, tell me, what's going on with … Amir and Almog?"

Lehava smiled. "Why are you asking? "What's up?"

"I was just curious." Esther redirected her gaze towards the binder.

"Their dad returned to Israel. He has some business to take care of. But he found them a house here, something truly amazing. A first-floor apartment with two bedrooms and a living room. It's stunning. And guess what? It's not even far from your parents' house. Maybe it's best not to mention it to your parents," she laughed.

Esther remained silent. After a moment, Lehava said, "If you want the number, look at the *Minitel*. Input the name "Amir Levy" into the search bar and search.

Esther nodded.

"Why are you sitting there like that?" Lehava asked. "Find the number and call. What are you waiting for? Would you rather do it at home with your parents?"

"But what am I going to say?" asked Esther. She got up from the chair and started pacing around the small room.

"Esther, please stop. You're making me feel nauseous. Dial his number and start a conversation. Why is that so difficult?"

Esther looked towards her father's office.

"He's in a meeting with his boss," Lehava reminded her. "You've got at least half an hour."

Esther approached the phone and dialed.

"Who is this?" asked a male voice on the other end of the line.

"It's Esther," she whispered.

"Esther! It's Amir. Did you miss me?"

She heard his smile across the line. "Lehava told me you had an apartment," she said. "So nice to hear. It seems it is close to my parents' home."

"Yes, we have an apartment. Would you like to come by and see it? We can meet Tuesday at noon, outside the kosher deli in Les Halles Mall."

As she hung up the phone, Esther's hand trembled.

"Let's hear about what's making you excited. So cute!" Lehava chuckled. "Like a kid in a candy store, dude. Take it easy, okay? Can you even take a seat? Here, take some money and get us something to drink," she said, and pulled some coins out of her pocket. "Bring me a coffee, okay?"

Esther skipped happily to the hot drink machine near the entrance of the *rabbinate*. She usually bought herself cocoa—Mom always warned against caffeine ("It'll stunt your growth," she said) but this time she decided she would buy a coffee. She put the coin in the slot and listened to it ring on its way down. Esther examined the menu with attention, not to be mistaken. She made her choice and pressed two buttons. The machine made a series of mechanical sounds, then filled a plastic cup like a small fountain. A minute or two later, Esther made her way back to the office with two brown plastic cups in her hands.

✐

The water droplets didn't bother Esther on the rainy afternoon. A white car stopped in front of her, and the window opened.

"Are you planning on coming?"

The passenger seat next to the driver was empty. Esther opened the door and got in.

"You're killing me with those kisses. These French people!" laughed Almog, who was sitting in the backseat.

"We have to do some business for a minute, Esther," Amir said. "Is that okay?"

"I thought the plan was to go to your apartment," Esther questioned.

The black clouds covered the sky. Without replying, Amir gently rested his hand on her thigh. She fell silent.

This time the street was lively. The sidewalks were bustling with people as merchandise-laden commercial vehicles were forcefully pushed together. "*So much color*", Esther thought.

This is what the heart of a capital city looked like. The business itself, however, looked like it did on her last visit. Even the long rolls of cloth had not moved.

They walked into the kitchenette and sat around a small square white table, a single step away from the bathroom door.

"So, what are you doing here? What business is this?" asked Esther.

"A clothing business," Amir said. He pulled a box of cigarettes out of the pocket of his brown leather jacket and lit a cigarette.

"Do you mind if I have a cigarette as well?" she asked.

"It's Marlboro. Are you ok with that?" asked Amir.

Esther nodded.

"Since when do you smoke?" Almog leaned over and lit the cigarette in her mouth. She blushed.

"Say, are you making coffee too?" laughed Amir. "I just bought black."

"No, I don't know how to make coffee." Esther's face was still red when she replied.

"What? Are you joking or what?" Amir got up from his chair. "Come on, baby," he motioned to Esther. "Do you see? It's a kettle, and it's coffee." He took out a bag of black coffee from the plastic bag he brought from the car. "Put a large teaspoon of coffee in a glass cup and add sugar. It's easy, isn't it? Simple. Stand here and learn." Almog watched them silently from his seat.

"That's all. Now you know how to make coffee," Amir announced, and sat back down in his seat.

"Where are you going?" Anabelle asked while sitting on the stairs.

Esther remained silent. She put a finger to her lips to signal her sister to be quiet. Sneaking out, she quietly closed the door.

Amir said he'd pick her up at the end of the street. Esther arrived early to keep him from waiting. When he arrived, they drove to his apartment. They entered the stairwell and went up to the first floor.

Amir opened the locked door and Esther followed him. When he sat down on the couch, she took a seat beside him.

"Where's Almog?" she asked.

"Went to get food," Amir said. "He'll be here in a moment. Are you hungry?"

"Not really," Esther admitted.

A hush filled the air. A moment later, the door opened.

"I brought shawarma!" declared Almog. "Oh, hey Esther."

The scent of lamb fat was overpowering in the living room.

"I didn't know you were coming, so I brought nothing for you," Almog said. "Would you like to eat mine?"

"I'm not that hungry. I'll eat some salad if you have it." Esther asserted.

She went to the little kitchen. The stove remained untouched. No one had ever used it. The walls were white and clean. Esther opened the kitchen cabinets and found the plates. They also appeared to be unused.

"Why did you bring plates?" asked Amir as she returned to the living room.

"I thought it would be more pleasant to eat on a plate, so it feels like home," she said.

"But we don't have to wash anything if we just use the wrappers," Amir said, highlighting how convenient it was.

"Can I throw the pickles and salad away, or should I put them in the fridge?" she asked as they finished.

"Throw them away," Amir said.

Esther collected the shawarma's yellow paper wrappers and went into the kitchen.

"What are you doing?" asked Almog. "I can throw paper in the trash, too."

"I know. I thought it would be nice to lend a hand."

She went to the sink and washed both glass plates.

"Want a cigarette?" asked Almog as she returned to the living room.

"Sure," she said. "But I'll make coffee first" she added and returned to the kitchen proudly.

She went back to the apartment three days later, and then two days after that. She tasted whiskey for the first time in her life and immediately had to run to the bathroom to throw up.

"Esther, I can't drive at the moment," Amir said one evening. "Would you like to spend the night here? Is that fine?" Esther nodded.

Later, the three of them got into bed together in an order that would be fixed from that night on.

First Amir got in, clinging to the windowsill, and turned his back on the others.

Esther followed him, wearing Amir's underwear and a cotton tank.

Finally, at the end of the bed, lay Almog.

Esther looked at him. He appeared alert, like he was about to bound over the white mattress like a spring. She turned around and faced Amir's back. She hoped he would turn to her and touch her, but he didn't.

The next morning, she made black coffee for all three of them. The aroma of freshly brewed coffee permeated the small apartment, intertwining with the lingering scents from the night's adventures.

Esther moved gracefully around the kitchen, the events of the previous evening playing in her mind like a reel of film. She couldn't deny the subtle shift in dynamics, the unspoken bonds that had formed during their shared moments.

"Mommy, Mom, Esther's home!" exclaimed Annabelle as Esther entered the house for the evening. She had been visiting the boys' apartment again as she had been for several weeks.

"Where have you been?!" asked Esther's mother. "I don't get why you keep coming back so late."

"I was hanging out with a friend," Esther said.

"Do I know her?" her mother asked.

"No," Esther was quick to reply.

"I don't approve of your behavior," Mom stated. "It's pushing the boundaries of what I can handle. I would love to meet this friend finally. I'm uncomfortable with you spending time like this with a stranger. You ended up spending the night again! It's quite disappointing." Mom said.

"Mom, can we please stop with the interrogations? I need to shower before Dad gets home," Esther said as she headed towards the stairs.

"Ask us for permission before you leave next time!" Mom cried after her. "You can't just vanish from here like that."

Esther looked at Annabelle in anger. The tension in the air was palpable as she climbed the staircase. The weight of her mother's disapproval lingered like a heavy cloud above her. The walls seemed to echo unspoken concerns.

Annabelle's innocent excitement clashed with the stern gaze of her mother. Esther couldn't shake the feeling that a chasm had widened between her and her family. It was a gap fueled by misunderstandings and unvoiced fears.

As the water cascaded in the shower, Esther let the droplets wash away the turmoil within her. The steam filled the bathroom, mirroring the fog that enveloped her thoughts. She had no idea this would test the bonds that tethered her to the familiar grounds of home. It would push her into the uncharted territory of what waited in her friend's apartment.

∽

Esther got up from the sofa in the apartment, grabbed her makeup bag, and sat on the floor in front of the mirror between the living room and the dining area. She pulled the lipstick out of the bag and swiped it across her lips. She then removed the sharp black pencil and stretched a fine line under her blue eyes.

Almog and Amir had finished a noisy argument, and she knew that staying quiet was the wiser choice.

Amir got up from the couch and went over to her.

"You're putting on makeup? Are you kidding?"

Esther smiled at him. "Sure, I'm heading out to buy some bread."

"Wait, so you're saying you gotta put on makeup for an hour just to get some bread?" he asked, not amused.

"Yes, why not?" she giggled.

"Well, go get bread. What's so funny?" he turned around. "And the next time you fold laundry, you don't have to leave it on the couch. What's the point? Are you trying to show that you've folded? Are you hoping for a reward?" Esther's tears halted inside her eyes, never making it to her cheek. She got up and went to the couch to take the folded laundry to their room.

When she came back to the living room, she saw Almog and Amir still on the couch. In Almog's hand was a rolled-up joint filled to the edges and rolled tightly around itself.

"Great stuff," Almog said.

Amir sighed and relaxed. "Hey Esther, wanna join us for a smoke?" he asked, cracking up. "It'll help you chill." He rolled around laughing.

Esther stared at them.

"What are you staring at? Are you shocked? Come on," Almog laughed.

On her way to the couch, Esther stopped in front of the mirror to check her reflection. She came to the couch and sat down between them. It was her favorite place in the world.

Amir handed her the joint. She turned it in all directions.

"Smoking, it's good for you."

Esther took a drag and started coughing.

"Pass it on to Almog. Why are you so stuck on it?"

Esther passed the joint to Almog and lay down on the couch with a smile on her lips. She thought her senses seemed to have sharpened. They hadn't.

In the morning, she woke up, still on the couch. In front of her was an ashtray with cigarette butts filling it like a pile of corpses. The room carried the remnants of a night that had blurred the lines between reality and haze. Esther found herself in a cocoon of disarray.

As she surveyed the aftermath, the echoes of Amir's words and Almog's laughter lingered in the air. The mirror reflected a face that had embraced the night's escapades. Esther couldn't help but wonder how these moments would ripple through the fabric of her existence. The joint had become a conduit, a passage to an altered reality that would shape her perceptions and redefine her boundaries.

✍

"Esther, I want to introduce you to someone. He is Israeli," Amir declared as he returned from one of his business trips to Israel.

"Who is it?" asked Esther.

"A mate," he said. "We're gonna grab dinner at the restaurant tonight, we'll chat there. Go get ready."

This time, Amir requested she sit in the backseat. She entered the car wearing the outfit he selected for her: a black minidress, black tights, and high heels. She had on blush, blue shadow on her eyelids, black under her eyes, and red on her lips.

"What's going on, Esther?!" Amir occasionally asked from the driver's seat.

"I'm OK."

Every time she answered, her voice held a tinge of sadness.

She looked out the window. This time she did not know where they were going, but the trip was longer than usual. When they arrived, she saw the restaurant as a shrine straight out of the Middle East. It was filled with dim lighting and gilded dishes adorned with lace-like engravings.

Amir and Almog made their way to a table in the restaurant's back corner, with Esther right behind them. Three men were waiting at the table. A handsome black-haired fellow got up from the chair and reached out to Esther.

"Esther, this is Uri," Almog said. "He's from Israel."

"Very nice to meet you," Esther said.

She scoured his appearance, noticing his big green eyes.

"Would you like to dance?" Uri asked her after they sat down.

Esther looked at the dance floor in the middle of the restaurant.

"Sure," she said.

They stepped onto the dance floor, and Esther grooved to the beat, twisting at the waist.

"Esther, can we talk? Come over here." Amir approached her, took her hand, and led her to the restaurant lobby entrance.

"Remember when you mentioned going back to Israel?" he asked.

"Yes, the first time we met." She whispered.

"You always bring up Israel in conversation." He added.

"Yes, it could be nice. Why are we even discussing this?" she asked.

"Long story short, you want to go back to Israel, don't you? You miss it so much, don't you?"

"Yes," Esther replied, confused about where the conversation was going.

"You should definitely go out with Uri. He'll bring you to Israel someday."

Esther froze in place.

"It will be worth it," Amir emphasized.

Esther looked down.

"That's what you're hoping for, right?" said Amir in a whisper.

"Yes," she whispered. "You know I …" Amir cut her off before she could finish.

"Esther, I'm staying in France, and I have a business to run, so you better be grateful. Esther, come on let's go! They're waiting for us... it's not cool. And remember what I told you, alright? Do me a favor and think about it."

When they returned to the table, Amir shook his head at Uri, who gave him a smile back.

The restaurant buzzed with a mix of laughter and conversation, but Esther felt an undercurrent of emotions surging within her. As she looked on the dance floor, the flickering lights mirrored the uncertainty in her heart. Amir's revelation about Uri and his wishes for her had a negative impact on the evening. She felt conflicted. The distant strains of music intertwined with the weight of Amir's words created a symphony of emotions that echoed in her mind.

"Esther, will I see you tomorrow at Amir and Almog's place?" Uri inquired as the evening ended. "I have some business with them," he added.

She looked at Amir and then back at Uri. "Maybe," she said.

Uri and his two friends arrived at the apartment the following afternoon. Esther waited in the living room as they sat in the kitchen and chatted.

Uri came out of the kitchen to join her on the couch.

"So, how are you? Is everything fine?" Uri asked.

"Yes, I'm ok," Esther said. She glanced into the kitchen.

Uri suddenly leaned over, grabbed both of her hands, and kissed her on the mouth. She tried to slip away, but he was too strong. He shoved his tongue into her mouth.

"Hey!" she said as he pulled away.

"What's the matter? We are a couple, right? said Uri.

Esther looked at him. The feeling of anger and fear that filled her body vanished. His warm body against hers felt pleasant.

She sent another look toward the kitchen. Amir was standing in the doorway.

"Is everything okay?" he asked Uri. "Are you having any issues with her?"

"No, she's fine," Uri replied.

He grabbed Esther's hand and pulled it after him into the small bedroom used by Amir and Almog's younger brother when he came to visit. Uri sat down on the bed covered with a plaid blanket.

"Don't be ashamed, come on!" he said.

He stretched out on the bed, undid his pants, and gestured for Esther to come closer. She sat down on the edge of the bed.

"Lie down!"

Uri stroked her slender legs.

"Wow, you're so beautiful! So, we're a couple, yeah?"

"Sure," Esther said, still unsure.

She pinned her legs together and looked at the ceiling.

"Tell me about Israel," she said.

He didn't answer, and she didn't want to talk any longer, either.

When he clung to her and moved against her leg, she thought of Amir.

"Well, I have stuff to take care of," he finally said. He walked out of the room and went back to the kitchen.

The air in the small bedroom lingered with a mix of vulnerability and confusion.

Esther's gaze remained fixed on the ceiling. The weight of the moment settled into the fabric of her reality. Uri's actions had stirred a whirlwind of emotions, leaving her grappling with the blurred lines of consent and the echoes of Amir's presence. The distant hum of conversation in the kitchen underscored the dissonance within Esther, who found herself at the crossroads of intimacy and uncertainty.

"My uncle wants to meet you," Uri told her a few days later. "You're going to be there, right? Because we're a couple, right, Esther?"

Since they arrived in France, Uri and his older brother had been living in their uncle's apartment on the sixth floor of a tall, modern, white building.

Surrounding the shopping center were buildings of different shapes and ages. Esther's mom would take she and Annabelle to the bookstore before the school year began at that same center.

Uri met her at the building entrance like they had planned and went up together. He opened the door without knocking.

In the corridor, three girls dressed up like fancy puppets caught Esther's eye. They were dressed up even though there was no holiday nor Shabbat. On each of their heads was a giant white ribbon, reminding Esther of Easter chocolate eggs. Two of the girls were tall and thick. Esther couldn't guess their ages. They and their little sister, who was also round, approached Esther. They touched her hair, walked around her, and even sniffed her.

"She is so beautiful," one marveled. "What's your name?"

"Her name is Esther," Uri replied with conviction. "Come on, leave her alone. You think she's something new for you to play with?"

"Who's that?" Esther heard a shout from the kitchen.

"Uri and his girlfriend," replied a bald, fat man sitting on the couch in front of the TV. It was Uri's Uncle Leon. He put his feet on the table next to a bowl of crackers.

"Do you know Zahava Ben?" Uri asked her.

"No," said Esther.

Take a seat," he said. "We're watching this movie called 'Drop of Hope.'"

The atmosphere in the apartment was strange. There was a blend of clashing energies and awkward encounters.

Esther found herself amidst the curious scrutiny of Uri's relatives. Each one expressed an opinion of her like spectators watching a carnival sideshow.

Uncle Leon's living room bore the marks of casual neglect. It held scattered crumbs and a faded ambiance from the bluish glow of the television. Esther couldn't shake the feeling she was on exhibit under the watchful gaze of those who deemed her entrance significant.

The encounter with the ribboned girls left a surreal impression. Their fascination with her created an aura of strangeness that lingered.

Amid the cacophony, Uri's voice cut through, raising questions about Zahava Ben, a name unfamiliar to Esther. The dynamics of the room mirrored the complexities of Esther's growing relationships. She felt entangled in the web of Uri's family. Uncertainty overshadowed the prospect of understanding and acceptance.

"Are you heading back to your parents' house from here?" Uri inquired as they exited his uncle's house and returned to the lobby building.

"Yes," Esther replied, placing her back against a ceramic-tiled wall Esther replied.

In a sudden motion, Uri seized her hand, urging her to follow him.

Ignoring the elevator, he opened the door to the staircase. Sunlight streamed in through the roof hatch illuminating walls adorned with brick sketches. Together, they climbed several floors.

When they reached the last story before the rooftop, Uri pushed Esther down and laid her on the cold floor. For a moment, he stood over her and watched her from above. He then kneeled at her feet, raised her hands above her head, and held them hard. She forced herself to smile. When he let her hands go, she left them there anyway. He unbuttoned her pants, rose above her, and rolled them down to the bottom of her calf. Then he deliberately reached for her underwear and pulled at them slowly.

Esther felt embarrassed and tried to resist but he pushed her to the dusty floor again. She surrendered.

He looked between her legs causing her to blush. He then lifted her shirt, pulling her tiny breasts out of her bra, and pressed his thumbs on the nipples.

Without pausing he unzipped his pants, lowered them to his knees, and revealed his penis. Esther stared at him. He massaged his limb using his right hand, moving it back and forth. His face turned red. Esther directed her gaze elsewhere.

He stopped abruptly, took off his pants, spread her legs, and penetrated her. He groaned, sweat rolling down his face.

The sensation of sharp glass cutting into her overwhelmed Esther. A scream erupted from her throat and her eyes filled with tears. The dirty stairwell moved up and down around them. Uri pressed his hand against her mouth while biting his lips. She closed her eyes. He increased the speed of his thrusts, panting and moaning. Finally, the hot liquid poured from her body into hers.

He stood up and picked up his pants. "That's it, I opened you up! I f-ed you," he proclaimed, patting her on her back.

∽

Esther returned home to find her father in a furious state, standing in the center of the living room.

"I just received a notice in the mail from the authorities. We need to go to the police station," he cried, waving a paper in his hand.

"What have you done?" "What happened?" asked Annabelle. "Why the police? This is so scary!"

"I haven't spoken to you, Annabelle," her father said. "I am talking to Esther. Come on, put on a coat. We're going right now."

As they rode the bus in silence, Esther felt as if each minute dragged on for hours. She noticed an unusual warmth in her underwear.

Esther sat down on the bench while her dad entered the first office, where the door was wide open. "Come," he ordered. Esther went with him to the detective's office, who had called them in for questioning. Her heart was thumping in her chest.

"Are you aware that your daughter is hanging out with criminals?" The detective behind the metal table asked after they sat down in front of him. Esther noticed rust on the table's corners.

"I don't understand," her father said. "What are you talking about? Esther, do you know what this is about?"

The detective looked at Esther. "What are they up to?"

"I don't know," Esther said, laughing nervously. "I'm not involved in their business." She felt another warm sensation between her legs. Her mind was devoid of thoughts as her body attempted to process, overcome, and adapt.

"What makes you laugh?" cried the officer and slammed the table with an open palm. "Do you actually want to go to jail?"

"I can't help you," Esther said.

The policeman approached her father. "This time I'll let her go," he said, "but next time it won't end so well. Make sure you explain the consequences to your daughter."

Esther's father followed her down the gray hallway. "Esther, what's wrong with you?! This is serious! Don't you feel bad for doing that to your old man?"

"It's not about you," Esther said. "What part don't you get?"

"I'm your father," he said. "So, it IS related to me."

"This is my life," Esther said. "This has nothing to do with you. Go home. I'm going to hang out with my criminals."

"Didn't you hear what the detective said?" Her father said, annoyed. "Forget about going to those junkies. You better listen and come home now."

"I'm not going home," Esther declared.

"Do as you please, but be prepared to face the consequences," her dad warned, pausing at the entrance of the police station, and giving her a stern glance. Esther looked at him, then turned around and continued on her way.

∽

"What are you doing here?!" Lehava asked, surprised. "Don't you have school?"

"Hey, don't yell!" Esther said. Her voice turned to a whisper "My dad doesn't know I'm here."

"Wow, you came alone. You're all grown up now." Lehava smiled.

"Do you mind taking a break? I need to talk to you for a moment."

"What is happening Esther?" asked Lehava.

"My chest is killing me." Esther whispered and unzipped her jacket. Her gaze shifted downwards.

"Damn, your breasts have gotten huge," Lehava said. "When was your most recent period?"

"A long time ago," Esther said. "But my period was never consistent."

"I hope you're not pregnant!" Lehava exclaimed.

"What's pregnant?!" Esther took a seat in a chair next to Lehava.

"I'll give you some cash, go get a blood test," Lehava said. "There's a lab right here on this street."

Esther took the money with trembling hands. "What do you mean, pregnant? How is that even possible?"

"You don't know how to get pregnant?" asked Lehava. "Why weren't you careful? Seriously, you've never heard of condoms before. Or the pill?"

Esther shrugged.

Lehava sighed. "No way I am having this conversation with you. Just do a test. When you exit the building, make a left turn. There's a lab on the opposite side of the road. The sign will guide you. Also, get tested for AIDS."

Esther rushed down the *Rabbinate's* stairs and waved to the guard. He pressed a small button and the big door buzzed and opened.

Esther turned left and crossed the road. After a few steps, she came across the shop window. Above it, a large sign in red letters read '*Laboratory.*'

"Hi there, what can I do for you?" the woman behind the counter asked.

"I need to take a pregnancy test," Esther whispered.

The woman handed Esther a questionnaire and a pen. "Do you have an identification document?" she asked.

Esther removed the ID card from her bag and handed it to the woman with trembling hands.

"Answer the entire questionnaire," the woman demanded.

Esther sat down on one chair in the waiting room and pulled the cap off the blue pen. Under the section titled "The reason for testing," she marked X in the boxes for "Pregnancy" and "AIDS." Cold sweat covered her body.

When she returned with the questionnaire, the clerk told her that payment needed to be made before the test. Esther used Lehava's money for payment.

"Take a seat now. Your name will be called when it's your turn." Esther took the magazine that was lying there on a small table and started flipping. She couldn't focus enough to read so she looked at the pictures and skimmed the headlines. Every few seconds, she raised her head towards the lab door.

A few minutes later, her name was called to begin her testing.

∞

"The results will be ready in three days," the clerk informed her, as she exited the room with a piece of cotton gauze pressed to her arm. "Where would you like us to send the results?"

"I'll come back to get my results, thank you," Esther replied, shaking as she walked onto the Parisian Street.

She spent the next few days alone within her room. Esther felt like a frightened fly circling and desperately searching for an open window.

The hours dragged on. Each minute was an eternity as she waited for the results to come back.

She moved mechanically from one classroom to another at school, scarcely paying attention to the teachers' words. Concentration had never been her forte, yet for now, school provided a refuge. It had become a sanctuary from her parents, sister, and especially Uri.

After the final school bell rang, she returned home. She made a hasty excuse to retreat to her room, feigning a load of homework. While there might have been some assignments needing her attention, she didn't care. They didn't matter.

Following dinner with her family, she excused herself, citing fatigue, a genuine sentiment. She felt fear, shame, and a profound loneliness. Her emotions lingered like unwelcome shadows.

ආ

Three days had passed, and it was finally time to head to the lab.

The clerk, a new face this time, moved like a sloth as she searched the drawer marked with 'results' in red.

"Here," said the woman, handing Esther a white envelope with the word "paid" stamped diagonally across it.

Esther dropped the envelope into her bag and left in a hurry. She needed to get far enough away from the *Rabbinate* so that no one would see her. She paused at a corner a few yards away, perfumed with dog urine, and nervously opened the envelope.

"HIV test—negative," the white paper read. Esther exhaled and closed her eyes. She moved on down the page.

"Pregnancy test—positive." Vomit rose up into her throat. She sat down on the sidewalk and burst into tears.

Esther crumpled the white paper, intending to toss it into a nearby garbage can. Hesitating, she changed her mind and tossed it back into her bag.

A few pedestrians shot her curious glances. She quickly got up and crossed the street and boarded a bus. It was the same stop she had shared with her father a few months earlier.

The bus was headed to the Gare du Nord train station. It gave her mind time to wander as the city passed by. During her first solo bus ride, she hadn't relaxed, fearing she might miss her stop. But this time she knew the route well. The familiarity gave her a certain reassurance. She placed her palm on her belly, smiling at first. Then the reality hit once again, and her tears highlighted how alone she was.

Finally arriving at home, she ducked into the bathroom to freshen up and hid her purse in a dark corner of her closet. She headed downstairs to join her mother in the kitchen, forcing a smile onto her face.

She ate dinner cautiously that evening, chewing each bite slowly and drinking more water. As she settled into bed, tears streamed down her face until exhaustion won out and allowed her to sleep.

The next morning, Esther awoke and made her way to school. Midway through her bus ride regret began to gnaw at her.

Stepping off the bus with the rest of the high school students, she walked with them down the boulevard. Instead of continuing towards the school gate, Esther made an impromptu decision. She turned right and headed in the opposite direction towards the bus station. She knew that bus number 5 would take her to the mall. From there, it would be a short walk to Uri's uncle's place.

"Esther, what are you doing here?" asked Uri as he opened the door.

"I have something to tell you," Esther replied nervously.

"So, what is it?"

Esther directed her gaze towards the floor of the stairwell. He hadn't invited her in yet.

"Come on, just say it," he said, getting annoyed.

"I'm pregnant." She whispered, making sure no one would hear her.

"You sure it's mine?" Uri asked with anger.

"Yes, look. Look at this," she said, handing him the creased paper. "The test is positive, you see, right?" She pointed at the paper.

"I can't read French."

"That's what it says," Esther said.

"You sure it's mine? Are you sure?"

"What do you mean?" stuttered Esther. You were the first time for me. You know I never …"

"That doesn't mean I was the last." He replied coldly.

She burst into tears.

"Alright, let's head downstairs," Uri said. They went down to the lobby.

"I don't know what to do," Esther muttered, sitting on the floor. "My parents will kill me. They're religious."

Uri approached Esther and stood beside her. "Keep the baby," he stated. "We'll be fine."

She looked at him. "Really?" she asked.

"Yes, definitely," he confirmed. "I have to go. My uncle's waiting. We'll talk soon." He kissed her on the head before heading to the elevator.

The thought of going back to school seemed ridiculous to Esther. Should she go home? That seemed impossible, too. She finally went to Lehava's house and rang the bell under the *Mezuzah*. Lehava seemed both reluctant and surprised to see her.

"Come on," she shouted. "We need to talk."

Esther stood at the entrance while Lehava went from the living room to the kitchen, and then to the children's rooms.

"Why are you standing there like that?" she finally asked. "Take a seat in the living room or whatever. I'll join you soon. Sorry, hon, I'm occupied with the kids."

Esther sat down on one of the black chairs.

Lehava finally finished with her kids and came back to the living room. She sat down facing Esther. "Tell me what's up. You're not visiting as often as you used to" she said.

"You were right," Esther said.

"What do you mean? What did I get right? Are you talking about the test?"

"Yes," Esther replied, with a lump in her throat.

Lehava turned her face away. "So, you're pregnant? What are you going to do?"

"I had a conversation with him, and he wants us to keep the kid."

Lehava stood up and left the room. Esther followed her to the kitchen, where Lehava began washing the dishes in silence.

"Why didn't you tell me?!" she erupted suddenly.

"Tell you what?" asked Esther.

"That you slept with him," Lehava said.

"I'm not sure," Esther said. "It was my first time."

"Oh?" asked Lehava.

Esther had tears in her eyes.

"Why'd you keep that from me? And why didn't you let me know afterwards? After you slept with him?"

Esther felt as if she were a child being scolded.

"I'm your bestie, aren't I?"

"I don't know why I didn't tell you," muttered Esther. "But that's how it went. I had blood in my underwear afterward."

"You should've shown me the blood. Did you tell anyone?" Lehava asked.

Esther was silent.

"I didn't expect it to happen, you know. It wasn't planned." Esther whispered.

"Esther, the first time needs to be planned down to the smallest details. It's essential to talk with your partner beforehand and agree on when and where. This is not a light matter. I hoped you would talk to Uri before doing it. I remember my first time. I bought beautiful underwear, and we picked a cozy place for a picnic beforehand. Esther, I thought you were going to date my nephew Almog. He is so gentle and smart."

"Lehava, I told him I was a virgin when we first met. He was the first guy I had ever had a relationship with. I kissed him once or twice before, but we didn't ever talk about having ..."

"Enough with the tears," Lehava interrupted her. "It doesn't matter anymore."

Lehava sighed and put her arms around Esther. "I wish you had told me. It's late. Let's get some sleep. I'll get you a pillow and a blanket."

Lehava disappeared into the darkness of the hallway.

Esther stood at the apartment entrance and took off her shoes.

"You can sleep on the couch. Tomorrow, you'll figure out what to do with Uri. Goodnight," said Lehava as she turned off the light.

"Good night," responded Esther. She sat in the darkness looking out the window.

She looked through the window of the door leading to the little balcony. Memories of the time she first met Lehava and her family came flooding in. Memories from when she used to babysit the kids. During those evenings, Lehava and her husband would head out to play cards at the casino or dine at a restaurant. Esther enjoyed spending time with Lehava's three young sons, opting for playtime over sleep. There was one memorable day when their roughhousing got so spirited that they broke the wooden frame of the bed.

After the kids were asleep, Esther would retreat to the small balcony. There she'd smoke in quiet, taking in the night air and the stars. One time as she was re-entering the apartment, strong winds slammed the door shut. She couldn't make it open against the force of the wind. It finally gave way, and she was relieved to be back inside. Closing the balcony door behind her, a sudden explosion-like sound startled her. Rushing to the kitchen, she discovered the window had shattered into pieces.

At that moment Lehava and her husband burst through the entrance, laughing until they saw Esther's distressed face.

"I don't know what happened, I swear," she cried. "All the window pieces are inside the kitchen sink."

"Oh my God!" exclaimed Israel.

"Are you okay, Esther?" Lehava asked.

"Yes," she responded. "Let's clean up the mess."

It was one of so many memories that raced through her mind as Esther laid her head on the sofa. She closed her eyes and fell asleep in her clothes.

A few weeks had passed since receiving the results of the pregnancy test.

Uri stood in the meat department digging around inside one of the refrigerators.

"What are you looking for?" asked Esther.

He shot her a look that made her stop talking. He grabbed an expensive pack of steaks. After checking the expiration date and smelling it, he looked around, and stuffed the steaks in his coat pocket.

Esther froze. She was about to freak out.

"Now it's your turn," Uri ordered.

"How?" Esther asked.

"I had hoped you were paying attention to me." He pushed her towards the fridge with the meat.

"But I'm not wearing a coat," Esther whispered.

"You've got a purse. That will work. Do it quickly and make sure you don't get caught, otherwise it's the end for you."

They rushed out of the store without going past the cashiers. When they went through the automatic door, Esther's legs almost gave way. Her mouth tasted like vomit.

"What are you doing?" Uri scolded her. " Do you think we did this for me? We got steaks for you, so you can eat something. You're pregnant, aren't you?"

They escaped without getting caught by the security guards.

"I'll cook you that steak before my uncle gets back home. You need to eat something," he said, taking her hand as they headed to the train station. This time, he had two tickets, so she wouldn't need to jump the turnstile. He handed one ticket to Esther, saying, "Take it. I don't want my baby to get hurt." A big smile stretched across his face. "Besides, a few days ago, they caught my brother and me sneaking aboard. It was a nightmare."

She fell asleep during the train ride to his uncle's apartment, her face against the smudged window.

❧

"Esther, wake up!" Uri yelled, and they got off the train just before the doors closed automatically. As they made their way down the stairs, they were met by a few police cars waiting for them by the side. Police officers emerged from their vehicles.

"You are under arrest!" one of them shouted after calling Uri by his last name. The police officers arrested him.

Esther collapsed on the stairs.

"This is my boyfriend!" she cried, "I'm pregnant."

"Calm down, ma'am," the officer told her.

"No one cares that you're pregnant!" Uri yelled defiantly as they placed him in the police car.

❧

"Where are you going again?!" her father's voice echoed through the room, laden with frustration, as Esther stood by the door.

She turned towards him, avoiding eye contact, and doing her best to conceal her baby bump.

"I need you to understand that this house, my house, is not a pedestrian crossing. Your behavior is not acceptable for your mom or me. Esther, who do you think you are?"

The intensity of her father's yelling struck Esther, causing her to remain silent momentarily. Her mother emerged from the kitchen, drawn into the unfolding confrontation.

"It's none of your business," Esther retorted, a spark of defiance in her voice. "I'm the one who decides where I'm going."

Her father, escalating the tension, stepped up, waving his fist in the air. Her mother intervened, placing a calming hand on his shoulder to interrupt the brewing storm.

"With this behavior, she's not welcome to live here," her father declared. Esther was caught in the crossfire.

Her father continued his barrage, questioning her choices.

"How can you come and go like this, never sleeping at home? Only prostitutes don't have the luxury of sleeping at home."

The weight of judgment hung in the air. His heavy accusations felt like a sharp sting.

"Esther, do you think we are foolish? The school contacted us to let us know you are skipping school. You're ruining your life!" her dad screamed.

Esther could no longer stand the strain of the situation. She turned around, her hand on the doorknob, bracing herself for what lay beyond.

"If you leave now," her father warned, his tone foreboding, "don't even think about coming back. Do you hear me?!"

Esther's mother hesitated, caught between loyalty to her daughter and a desire for peace. "Be quiet," she finally urged, her voice a fragile plea.

Esther's resolve remained unshaken. Without looking back, she opened the door and stepped out into the unknown.

As she stepped into the cool night air, Esther felt a mix of fear and determination. The weight of her choices pressed heavily on her shoulders, but a glimmer of independence fueled her steps forward. The city lights beckoned her, and she walked into the uncertainty of her future, leaving behind the echoes of familial disapproval.

Esther ventured out to the quiet, dead-end street; none of her neighbors were in sight. She turned to the right to catch the bus, stopping at the station in front of the bakery and waited. Occasionally, she glanced back at the street corner, hoping her dad or mom would appear. They didn't. Only a few strangers passed by. She continued to wait for what seemed like an eternity until the bus arrived.

The journey to Uncle Leon's apartment wasn't long. Soon, she would find herself in Uri's arms.

Esther walked for a few minutes before arriving at the building. She hurried to the elevator, heading straight to Uri's uncle's apartment. She quietly knocked on the door hoping Uri would be the one to open it. The anticipation of being in his arms grew stronger with each passing moment.

"What the f- are you doing here?" Uri whispered, halfway closing the door.

"Can I come in?" she cried.

He opened the door, looked back, and said, "Come on in!"

Esther shut the door behind her. "I have nowhere else to go," she told Uri. "I can no longer live with my parents. I got kicked out and if they find out I'm pregnant, I'll be in even bigger trouble. Lehava is angry at me. I can't go back to Amir's house because you're my boyfriend, so that's not acceptable, right?"

"What happened to Lehava? I thought you guys were BFFs." He asked.

"I pissed Lehava off because I didn't tell her we had sex. She expected me to show her proof that I was a virgin before you."

"She's nuts. Who does she think she is?" Uri yelled. "I'll chat with my uncle," Maybe he'll let you crash with his daughters for a while. Remember, he's got three girls, you met them. He's obsessed with his girls."

"Yes, I remember. The youngest one really likes me." She smiled.

"Come on, are you stupid, Esther? The little one won't be sleeping with you, just the other two."

Esther forced a smile and whispered, "Ok, thank you so much."

Uri's aunt complied and placed two mattresses on the floor: one in the boys' room for Uri and the other in the girls' room for Esther. "Just to make it clear, this is temporary," she stressed.

On the first night, while everyone was asleep, Uri sneaked into the girls' room. He slipped in behind Esther and removed her pajama pants under the soft blue blanket.

"Stop," she whispered, and tried to turn her head. "There are kids around."

"Everyone's asleep. What are you worried about? I want you. Are you my girl or what?" Uri whispered back.

When he entered her, he covered her mouth with the palm of his hand. After a moment, he moaned and pulled out of her. He got up and went back to his room, saying nothing.

∽

"Good morning," Esther said. "I need …"

"What?!" Aunt Sylvie turned from the stove.

"I need a shirt."

"Why?" Aunt Sylvie asked.

"I have to go," Esther replied.

"Where are you going?" Where is Uri?"

"Uri has some business with his brother. He gave me money so I could go job hunting." She said smiling.

"Finally, a piece of good news," Sylvie said. "He's right. Since you have French citizenship, you are eligible to work. He's got nothing, poor guy. He can't speak French and doesn't have a job."

Aunt Sylvie turned to the eldest daughter's room and Esther followed.

"I'm looking for a nice long-sleeved shirt," Esther said. "It looks more serious."

Sylvie gave her a shirt that was several sizes too big. "Be careful with it and don't forget to bring it back!" she warned.

"Thanks, I'll give it back. I won't forget," Esther said with a smile as she went to another room to change before heading out.

Esther, wearing her oversized clothing, glanced at her reflection in the shop window before walking to the supermarket.

"Good morning, I'm Esther. Nice to meet you."

"Good morning," said a short old man holding a cup of hot coffee. "What do you want?"

"I was wondering if you're looking for cashiers?" she asked, still standing in the entrance of the store.

"Have you ever done this before?" the manager asked, questioning her with his gaze,

"No, but I'm a fast learner and very hardworking." she answered.

"I'll be generous and offer you a three-day trial," the manager stated. "If you're alright, we'll start payment. What do you think?"

"It's going to be great," Esther assured. "When can I begin? I really need the money. My boyfriend and I are ..."

"At 7:00 a.m. sharp, tomorrow. Don't be late."

When she showed up the following day, the manager passed her a thick binder. "Memorize all the barcodes," he instructed.

Esther spent the next few days scanning barcodes and organizing shelves. On the fourth day, she took her place behind the cash register with confidence, dressed in a red jacket.

She had a proper job and a real salary. She was expecting a child with Uri. Soon, she would fulfill her lifelong dream of becoming a mom. Soon they would have enough money to move to their own place. "Everything's going to be alright," she thought and smiled.

"We're heading out today," Uri told Esther when she got back from work, tired and proud. "Amir and Almog are throwing a party with all their partners." He grabbed her hand and dragged her to the girl's bedroom.

"Wait, I'm exhausted. I barely ate anything today," Esther said.

"There's going to be plenty of food at the party. Make it quick and wash up. On the way, we'll stop by Catherine's, my brother's friend. She'll let you borrow a stunning outfit." he said.

"Uri, we need to talk. I thought we'd be in our own place by now. It's difficult for me to sleep on this mattress and you said …"

Uri grabbed her by the mouth and squeezed hard.

"Be grateful. Do you really think we can move with your tiny salary? Go get ready," he said, taking his hand off her mouth and kissing her forcefully.

Esther, clad in tight black leather pants and a black corset, clung to Uri, shadowing him like a frightened animal. Uri casually passed a hand down the side of her body, his touch lingering on her chest.

"There's food over there," he pointed out. "Go. You said you were hungry. I'll take care of you after that." He grabbed Esther's hand and mischievously placed it on the front of his pants. She jerked her hand away from his pants and hurried over to the table. There was a mouthwatering spread of hummus, crackers, fruits, veggies, cheese, and charcuterie.

She returned from the table, finding Uri sitting on a couch next to a young woman.

"When can we split and go home?" Esther whispered in Uri's ear, presenting a plate overflowing with goodies. "I'm tired and have an early shift tomorrow."

"Esther, I'm busy talking to someone," Uri scolded her. "Be cool and say hi." His voice was nearly overpowered by the loud music.

"Hello. I'm sorry, but I need to get some sleep. Uri, you know it is one symptom of the …"

"It's too late," Uri impatiently stated, without glancing at her.

Esther looked at the red-haired girl next to him.

"We missed the last train and have no way of getting home. If you're feeling tired, go find a spot to lie down."

Uri resumed his conversation with the woman leaving Esther to weave through the dancing guests. The crowded room, pulsating music, and a blend of cigarette smoke and perfume gave her a headache. She wondered if Amir and Almog were present but couldn't spot them.

Esther ventured into the villa in search of a quiet space. Opening one door, she found herself in the restroom and used it; she always needed to pee. After a moment, she opened another door, this time leading to a bedroom. Esther had finally found a bed with a real and comfortable mattress. Closing her eyes, she thought of Amir and Almog, missing them dearly. She smiled and fell asleep; it had been a long time since she had slept on a proper bed.

While she slept, she started experiencing sickness. She felt the bed moving up and down, slow then fast.

Someone was groaning.

Esther's eyes opened to the sight of the red-haired girl lying beside her, smiling as weird sounds came from her mouth. The stranger opened her mouth wider while loud moans escaped it.

Uri was on top of her, the bed shaking.

"Keep going, keep going," the girl sighed in French. Uri, fully immersed, did not acknowledge Esther.

Disgust overwhelmed her, and she almost threw up.

She rushed out into the hallway, opened the bathroom door, and vomited. She sat on the floor for a minute, then turned on the faucet to clean up.

Regaining her composure, she returned to the bedroom. She found Uri and the red-headed girl sitting on the edge of the bed.

Enraged, she attacked Uri, pouncing on him. "What did you do?" she yelled, delivering a punch to his chest.

Uri grabbed her fists. "What are you talking about?" he said casually. "Chill out."

"I'm having your baby, and you're sleeping with that … woman!" she spat, lunging toward the red-haired girl.

Uri grabbed her arm and pulled her back. "Relax, we did nothing," he said. "You were dreaming. Get ready. You need to head to work and not get fired."

Esther, still in her party clothes, left in search of the train station, the night's events lingering in her mind. The unfamiliar streets and the weight of her personal struggles as she made her morning commute added to the surreal experience.

The store manager strolled up to Esther as she made her way back from the bathroom. "Everything alright?" he asked, genuine concern etched on his face. Esther shifted her gaze and muttered, "I'm okay."

"You sure about that? You've been in and out of the bathroom like five times already this morning," he pointed out, raising an eyebrow.

Esther's eyes fell to the less-than-impressive flooring as she confessed, "I'm pregnant."

The manager's eyes widened in surprise.

"Wait, you've been here a month and a half, and you're dropping this bomb now? Are you messing with me? What's going on?" His tone was a mix of disbelief and frustration. "Unfortunately, if you're pregnant, you can't keep working here. "He turned around and began walking back toward his office, leaving Esther standing there, her secret out in the open.

"Hand in your jacket and badge. Just leave them in the break room. Oh, and don't count on a paycheck this month." His parting words hit hard, a brutal reality settling over Esther. As he accused her of dishonesty, he added insult to injury, shouting, "You're such a liar!" The door slammed shut, leaving Esther alone, shattering her dignity.

Tears streamed down her pale cheeks, reflecting the sadness within. The suddenness of the situation left her reeling and struggling to grasp the magnitude of the changes unfolding. In the silent aftermath, Esther stood in the stark hallway, a sense of isolation enveloping her.

Esther peeled off the badge, its black letters spelling out her name.

Nabila, the other cashier, expressed her sympathy, saying, "I'm so sorry this is happening to you. I wish I could do something for you."

Esther remained silent and slowly made her way to the break room. She placed her badge on the worn table, its surface bearing the marks of many such disheartening encounters. Her red jacket, a symbol of her role in the store, found a temporary refuge on a chair in the small, dirty room.

Esther stepped out of the store and found herself amidst the bustling streets teeming with people and cars. The urban symphony played around her. Life continued its relentless pace ignoring her. The contrast between the external world's vibrant energy and her internal turmoil was stark.

She took a moment to clean her face and compose herself. The cool breeze carried away the last traces of tears. She took a deep breath, steadying her emotions. Her thoughts turned to Uri, the one person who had been a constant source of support.

Pondering what to say to him, Esther couldn't help but reflect on the abrupt turn her life had taken. She grappled with a mixture of emotions—disappointment, frustration, but also a spark of determination.

As she pushed through the sea of self-absorbed people, Esther began piecing together what she would say to Uri. "I lost my job" she whispered.

"Would you like to marry him?" one of Uncle Leon's daughters asked Esther.

It was late at night, and the girls were already lying in their twin bunk beds in the hushed stillness of the room.

"Yes, of course, I want to marry him. I want a wedding and a white dress like in the movies," Esther replied. Her voice carried the dreams that filled her mind as she lay on her mattress on the floor.

"Are you in love?" the younger sister inquired, her curiosity cutting through the quiet.

"Of course, we are in love," Esther asserted with a gentle smile. "We are going to have a wedding with a big white cake and lots of food," she continued. Her words resonated with certainty. She was on the verge of nodding off, but continued, sharing her dream. "I can already picture it."

"So, when's the wedding?" the two girls asked together, leaning over their bunk beds, and peering down at Esther with eager anticipation. "Can we be the bridesmaids?" they chimed in unison.

"Yes, of course, you can," Esther replied, her warmth embracing the excitement of the moment. "I don't know the wedding date yet, but hopefully soon," she promised. The prospect of the future continued to shape their imaginations.

"Why soon?" Has he already proposed to you? Where is the ring?" The girls pressed further; their curiosity now tinged with impatience.

"Because of the baby," Esther revealed. It was a surprising revelation.

The oldest girl leaned over the side of the top bunk bed, her eyes widening in disbelief. "What, are you pregnant?!" she asked incredulously. The bombshell had caught them off guard.

"Yes," Esther calmly confirmed. "Now go to sleep. It's late," she gently admonished with finality. She had had enough of the nighttime conversation filled with dreams and surprises.

〜

"Mom, guess what? She is pregnant!" Exclaimed the eldest daughter the next morning during breakfast.

"They're not married yet," the little sister added. "Isn't that forbidden?!"

Aunt Sylvie placed the pan on the stove. "Who's expecting, dammit?!" she asked in a shocked tone.

"Esther told us last night that she was pregnant," replied the eldest, with her mouth full of scrambled eggs.

Aunt Sylvie's face turned red. "Leon!" She shouted out. "Come to the kitchen, it's a total disaster!"

Uncle Leon came in. "Hey, what's going on?" he asked.

"She's pregnant. That b-tch!" Aunt Sylvie yelled.

"What do you mean? Who told you that?" Uncle Leon asked.

"Your daughter told me. I brought a prostitute into my home."

"Dad, it's true, I swear," the eldest said. A little smile hung on the tip of her lips. "They are having a baby. Mom does that mean that …"

"Oh lord Leon, do something!" she cried out, interrupting her daughter, and collapsing onto a kitchen chair.

Uncle Leon took a slice of bread from the table and walked out of the kitchen to his armchair in the living room.

"Uri!" he shouted. "Get up and come to the living room ASAP." He saw Esther entering the room. "Alone," he added with an angry tone.

Uri walked out into the hallway. "You'll wait for me in the room, got it?" Uri yelled as he hurried past Esther. "Go to the bedroom, close the door and don't go anywhere", he said from the living room.

Esther pressed her ear against the door, attempting to listen.

"She can't sleep next to my daughters. "They're still virgins," Aunt Sylvie said, joining Leon and Uri in the living room.

"Chill out," Uncle Leon commanded. "Where are they? YOUR daughters?"

"I sent them to school, God bless them."

"Well, calm down. I'll find Uri and his pregnant girl-friend somewhere else to go."

Esther's hopes sunk.

"Where are we going to go?" she heard Uri's voice. "You are my only family." He added, almost crying.

"Quiet," said Uncle Leon. "I'll find a solution."

"And what about my poor innocent girls until you find one?" Aunt Sylvie yelled. "I don't want that garbage near my girls."

Uri laughed.

Esther sat down on the floor of the bedroom and tucked her head between her legs, resting it upon her small, round stomach.

"There's an empty storage shed downstairs. I'll look for a key and you can live there," Uncle Leon declared. "And now, I've had enough. I don't have time for this. I have business to take care of." He got up from his armchair and left the apartment.

∽

Uri and Esther found themselves adjusting to their 'new neighbors': a family of small gray mice. The mice shared the dark shed Uncle Leon had move them into. They gnawed the edges of the used mattress that Uri had found for them on the street.

There were no windows in the shed. Only a steel door that separated them from the reality outside. Uri had placed the mattress in the center of the space, along with a few other items. There were a couple candles, some matches, a half-full plastic water bottle, a packet of tissues, and two blankets. They had lived there for more than a week, but Esther had never seen the corners of the shed. Daylight did not reach them during the daytime through the open door, and at night the candlelight was too dim.

She lay beside Uri on the stained mattress, her blue eyes wide open in the dark.

"What's wrong with you? Not sleeping again?" complained Uri.

"I don't fall asleep well when it's so dark," Esther admitted.

Uri cursed under his breath. A moment later, she heard a match being struck. A white candle ignited and lit up the area around the mattress. "Here," he said, turning his back to her.

After they both had fallen asleep, the flame bit into the corner of the mattress. Thick smoke immediately filled the small space. Esther woke up coughing. The light of the flames illuminated the entire shed.

"Uri, Uri, wake up!" she shook him. Uri woke up complaining as he discovered the fire. He reached for the water bottle next to the bed and poured it over the flames. The fire went out. He lay back down on the sooty, wet mattress.

"Open the door," he ordered. "I can't sleep with this stink."

The next morning, the sun came up as usual. Last night's events had not seemed to change anything. Uri got up and went into his uncle's home to shower and eat.

While he was gone, Esther began airing out the space and checking to see what had burned.

When she lifted Uri's pants, she saw that they were stained with dry diarrhea. She dropped them and ran outside, throwing up next to a tree near the shed. She wiped her mouth on her sleeve and looked up at the kitchen window. She was hoping Uri would come back with something for her to eat.

When she woke up the next day, she was alone in the shed. The door was half-open. She stood up and removed the cobwebs above her. Suddenly the door opened wide. Uri was standing in the doorway.

"Take it," he said, tossing her a box with a blonde girl on the front. "I brought you hair dye. Blonde is what I love."

"You stole it," said Esther, looking at the box.

Uri looked at her menacingly. "What did you say?!"

Esther cringed. "Nothing," she said. "Sorry."

Uri walked over to the mattress, swung his leg around, and kicked her.

"Say thank you and shut your mouth, b-tch." He kicked her again and again on her legs, shoulders, and ribs.

"My baby!" cried Esther. She hunched over tightly, protecting her belly.

Uri swung his leg and kicked again.

"Whore!" he shouted. "I wish you'd lose that baby, got it? You need to color your hair blonde. Do you understand? I want to f- a blonde!"

The blows left Esther bruised, both physically and emotionally. The once hopeful flicker in her eyes was now replaced by a haunting darkness.

A while had passed after the beating and Esther remained on the mattress, staring apprehensively at the imposing iron door. It was the only thing standing between her and the outside world.

Convinced that Uri wouldn't be back soon, she cautiously turned her gaze back to the interior of the shed. She needed to find the glass jar he had been hiding.

After a brief but frantic search, she found it, removed the lid, and began feverishly pulling out coins. Esther took a deep breath and approached the hefty iron door. Summoning all her strength, she managed to pull it open. It creaked loudly as it opened, and she peered outside.

This was the time when adults headed to work, and children went to school. She waited, wanting to remain unseen. When the coast was clear, she slipped quietly into the street, crossing the courtyard, and blending into the shadows of the trees. She carefully navigated her way to the main road, glancing over her shoulder for fear that Uri might spot her from one of the windows. Reaching the street, she anxiously awaited the arrival of the bus while her mind raced.

"Are you going to Sarcelles Saint-Brice station?" she nervously asked the bus driver as he opened the doors. Receiving an affirmative response, she handed over the coins she had taken. He counted them before handing her a ticket.

"Please sit down," the driver instructed. Esther sensed his lingering gaze on her noticeably round stomach as she found a seat. Her teeth chattered as she surveyed her fellow passengers: a mother, a daughter, and a woman with a baby in a stroller.

The bus left and she did her best to distract herself. Gazing out the window at the passing buildings, she imagined the lives of those living within.

Each jolt of the bus sent a sharp pain through her ribs, interrupting her thoughts. The bus finally stopped in a familiar neighborhood. She got out and looked down the dead-end street. She hesitated. The thought of facing her parents filled her with trepidation. Maybe returning home wasn't such a good idea. But where else could she go?

Taking tentative steps towards the house, she froze. She thought about making a retreat to the main street. The internal struggle weighed heavily on her. She worried she might attract unwanted attention. She was unkempt and disheveled. It had been days since she last showered, and the pungent scent of her armpits lingered. She was a sight to behold in tattered clothing, her hair dyed an unnatural orange, and her protruding belly accentuating her fragile frame.

She clutched her bruised ribs as she tried to catch her breath. Minutes passed before she summoned the courage to proceed.

She knocked gently on Mrs. Afoua's door. She was her parent's neighbor. She hoped her mother wouldn't see her.

The wait felt like forever before the door opened. A look of surprise flickered across Mrs. Afoua's face as she scrutinized Esther. She grimaced before finally deciding what to do.

"Come in," she offered. "Nadia!" she called to her eldest daughter. When Nadia arrived, Mrs. Afoua exchanged a few words with her in Arabic before instructing her in French, "Take her to your room."

Esther and Nadia climbed the brown wooden staircase to the first floor. They settled on Nadia's bed, making small talk for a moment. Esther took in the pink wallpaper and, after a brief silence, began chatting once again.

They discussed topics typical of girls their age—singers, fashion, and recent songs. The only topic Nadia refrained from discussing was the subject of Esther's pregnancy.

"You'll be fine," she whispered softly. That was all Esther needed to hear.

Mrs. Afoua's voice echoed from downstairs. Esther knew deep down she had called her mother.

Esther walked into the hallway and stood at the top of the stairs. "Yes?" she responded.

"I talked to your parents," Mrs. Afoua said with a smile, her brown eyes glistening. "Don't worry; they're not mad. Come on, get down here and have some water."

Esther came down to the kitchen, where her neighbor handed her a glass of cold water.

"And now you better go," she suggested, taking the glass from her hands.

Esther stepped back onto the dead-end street of her childhood. She reminisced about afternoons spent with kids from the nine houses. Diverse backgrounds and religions, all playing baseball, soccer, or any other game. Listening to music from any one of the kids' rooms.

Mrs. Afoua didn't go with her. Instead, she closed the door behind Esther and went to her kitchen, watching Esther from behind the curtain.

Esther walked a few steps to the next house; her parents' house. The black gate with golden ornaments was open, so she entered the familiar front yard.

✑

The door of the house swung open, and her parents emerged to greet her in the middle of the path. Confusion and exhaustion enveloped Esther like a tidal wave.

"My daughter! My daughter!" her mother exclaimed, embracing Esther in a tight hug.

After a few moments, Esther stepped back, attempting to conceal her rounded belly.

"Do you want to eat something?" her mother asked as they entered their familiar and soothing home.

"No, thank you," Esther replied.

"Oh my God," cried Esther's mom, "Esther, we looked for you for so long. I asked Dad to drive around the neighborhood to look for you." Esther's mom continued, "We are so happy you're here."

Esther remained silent, recalling a time when she spotted her dad's car in the neighborhood where Uri's family lived. One afternoon, she saw her dad's car hidden behind a tree. She watched her mom looking out the car window, calling for Esther. Esther had said nothing.

"I'm going to sleep," she said as she began to climb the stairs.

"Yes, sure, go to sleep," her father said.

Esther made her way upstairs, finding her room as it was when she left. It was still adorned with black and white posters of young couples kissing passionately in the rain. She stroked the furniture with her left hand while her right hand rested on her round belly. Collapsing onto the bed, she gave in to her exhaustion and went to sleep.

"Esther!" her father called from downstairs after hearing water running in the upstairs sink. "Come on, we need to talk."

"Can I come too?" Annabelle cried from the next room.

"No, my sweetheart," their father replied. "It's a serious talk."

She came downstairs and took her place at the wooden table in the dining area with her parents. Her father started the conversation.

"So, what do you think we are going to do, Esther?" he began. "We must find a solution to your problem, and we need to fix what you've done."

Esther sat silently, perspiring. This was not going to go well. She finally resigned herself and spoke.

"All right," she said cautiously, anticipating her fate.

"Our financial situation will not allow us to help you raise a child," her father continued. Her mother had remained stoic and silent beside him.

"They are not married," her mother finally said.

"We will take care of everything," her dad said.

Esther knew what he meant by "taking care of everything." The weight of the decision hung heavily in the air.

The following day, Esther's mother took her to the OBGYN. From the moment they entered the clinic, Esther felt like she had become deaf. Not a single word that came out of the doctor's mouth got through to her.

After several unsuccessful attempts at conversation, Esther's mother answered instead.

Esther lay down on the bed and turned her face toward the white wall during the examination. She tried to hold back the tears, but the nausea and fatigue were too much. Her tiny body shrank. All she felt was devastation.

She recalled how a few years earlier she had asked her mother to go with her to the gynecologist. Her mother had refused.

The doctor covered the ultrasound device with gel and placed it onto Esther's belly. She held her breath. After a moment, Esther could hear a beating sound. It was a few seconds before she realized what she was hearing: it was the baby's heartbeat. She covered her ears with her hands to block it out.

"The fetus already has a pulse," the doctor said. "It's too late to have an abortion in France."

Esther looked at her mother, whose eyes were full of tears.

"Maybe in London they would be able to handle this situation," said the doctor. He handed Esther's mother a handwritten piece of paper.

"Here you go. There's an address and a phone number. Good luck."

Mom and Esther took the bus in silence. No one spoke during the entire 20-minute ride back to the house. When they arrived home, Esther went up to her room and cried. She had to say goodbye to her child. She needed to bid farewell before ever saying hello.

Esther longed to meet that child. She loved kids and had dreamt of being a mom since she was a little girl. She already loved him.

She was convinced it was a boy with green, gigantic eyes like his dad. As for the color of his hair, she wasn't sure if it would be like hers or like Uri's. She would never know. She hoped he wasn't afraid of his fate like she was. She hoped he couldn't understand what was going to happen. She hoped he was warm.

She had heard his little heart. The thought of stopping it was more than she could bear. She hoped he wouldn't suffer.

She hoped she could forget him, but deep down, she knew she never would.

"I talked to Lehava. She'll go to London with you to take care of … your problem," Esther's father said the next morning.

"You're not coming with me?" Esther asked.

"And leave your sister alone?" her mother responded. "She's not responsible for your actions, poor thing. And your dad has to go to work."

"But we'll pay for all the expenses," Esther's father was quick to say. "For the hotel room, the clinic, and the plane tickets for you and Lehava"

"You've already had a conversation with the clinic in London?" Esther asked.

"Yes, we did, and we had to borrow money to afford everything." Her mother blurted out.

Esther whispered, "I thought you would come with me."

"Mom needs to stay with me. You always wanted to have a boyfriend, and now look what happened. We all know how you got pregnant, Esther. We aren't idiots. This was always what was important to you—relationships with boys—and now here we are." Said Annabelle.

"What does that have to do with the fact that Mom won't come with me?" said Esther, devastated.

"That has to do with the fact that we are a Jewish religious family, and your dad is working at the *Rabbinate of Paris.* He has a lot of responsibility and a reputation to maintain in the community. You know that a respectable Jewish girl must be a virgin until she marries a Jewish gentleman. None of that will happen now, and all the good family options are no longer available. Your sister is still young, and I need to take care of her. But Lehava is your friend, isn't she?" said her mother.

"Yes, Mom. I'm going to head to my room to rest." Esther put her palm on her round belly and caressed it slowly before leaving.

That night, Esther weighed her options and realized she no longer had any left. She couldn't find the strength to run away again. Even if she had the strength, she had no idea where she could go. Returning to Uri would spell trouble, even danger. She was exhausted, physically, mentally, and emotionally. She spent the rest of the night talking to her belly, explaining the situation from all angles to her unborn child. At the end, she softly muttered, "I'm sorry."

A few days later, in the morning hours, they stood near the information center of a large hall at Orly Airport, waiting for Lehava. When she arrived, Esther's father handed her both passports and tickets, plus a bundle of cash. Her dad said goodbye and left for his office. Lehava and Esther boarded their plane.

Upon landing, a black taxi took them from the airport to a small house in central London. An elderly woman opened the door for them, politely swayed her head and led them to their room down a hallway covered with floral wallpaper.

"So scary!" declared Lehava as she sat down on one bed. "Your father gave me a lot of cash. I'm terrified of losing it."

That evening, Lehava did her best to lift Esther's spirits. She regaled her with amusing tales, transporting them back to the day they first met.

"Do you recall," Lehava reminisced, "when we were at the bakery next to the office? We grabbed a sandwich for lunch, and the baker asked, 'et avec ceci' (what else?). I thought she was trying to sell me some sausages. You couldn't stop laughing."

"We shared so many joyful moments," Lehava continued. "But now, let's rest. We have an early start tomorrow."

Despite Lehava's attempt to lighten the mood, Esther found it difficult to sleep that night. The impending abortion and the disconnection she felt from the child growing inside her consumed her thoughts. Worries gnawed at her. She had fears of the procedure, anxiety about the anesthesia, and concerns about her ability to conceive in the future. Then there was the lesser, but still daunting prospect of forgoing her beloved morning coffee and waking up the next morning at such an early hour. These thoughts swirled in her mind relentlessly.

She would not find sleep.

She couldn't hold back a yawn as they entered the discreet clinic the next morning. A nurse escorted them to a room, gave Esther a pink robe, and asked her to undress. Then they waited. The wait seemed to last for hours. Esther managed to find a position where her bruised ribs didn't bother her, and she almost fell asleep.

"I'm sorry I didn't believe you," Lehava said abruptly.

"What are you sorry about?" asked Esther.

"That he was your first time," said Lehava. She did not look at her but looked out the window at the fog-covered London Street instead.

"It's okay," Esther said. She put her arm across her face and almost fell asleep again.

"What the heck is this?!" Lehava exclaimed startling Esther as she was dozing.

She got up from her chair and went over to the bed, looking at Esther. "Why didn't you shave your legs and trim your nails?"

The expansive staircase within the clinic spiraled like a colossal snail. Its curves guided Esther and the accompanying nurse to the first floor. There was a chill in the air that enveloped her, seeping through her core.

An hour later the procedure was complete. She descended to the ground floor, arriving at the recovery room.

"It was a boy," disclosed an English-speaking nurse.

Esther grappled with the surreal notion that this might be a dream.

Lehava voiced her concerns and questions in broken English to the nurse. She sought guidance on the next steps for taking care of Esther.

The nurse reassured her. "You'll be able to take her home in a couple of hours. Everything went perfectly."

'Perfect' was not the word to describe it. Esther came up with a list of words to describe it, but perfection wasn't among them.

All that day and the following morning, Esther remained in bed.

"Well, let's get out already!" Lehava said impatiently. "Our flight back to Paris leaves tomorrow morning. You need some fresh air."

They took a bus through the city until they arrived at Lehava's chosen destination. It was a pretzel shop bearing a handwritten sign proclaiming, 'We speak Hebrew here." Esther didn't wish to speak at all.

The next morning Lehava and Esther found themselves enveloped in a cocoon of silence during their flight from London to Paris. Each was deep in their own thoughts and emotions. The constant hum of the airplane engines created a barrier between them.

When the flight attendant approached to take their drink orders, they both selected white wine. It was a subtle, unspoken connection amid their otherwise independent lives. Sipping from their respective glasses, they shared the confined space without exchanging a single word.

The landscape beneath them transformed as they crossed borders. The patchwork of fields and rivers gave way to the sprawling beauty of Paris as they approached from above.

Despite the shared experience of the journey, Lehava and Esther remained isolated from one another. Each of them lost in their individual world. Each absorbed in her own contemplations.

Upon arrival, a palpable shift occurred. The end of the flight marked not only the physical arrival in Paris, but an unspoken acknowledgment that their journey together was over.

The City of Lights beckoned to them promising new beginnings. The promise echoed silently between them as they ventured into the bustling terminal. Each woman absorbed in her own reflections marking the finale of their adventures.

☙

After returning to France, Esther's parents orchestrated a trip to the north to ease her recovery from both the abortion and her broken ribs.

"We're planning to visit my brother's house by the coast. You will need to rest. Plus, it will be good to get away from here for a bit," her dad suggested.

"Why would we need to get away?"

Her father responded, "Your friends came looking for you here, but I took care of them."

"What?!" Esther exclaimed.

"They won't be coming back," her father assured her.

Esther fixed him with a questioning gaze. "What do you mean?" she probed.

Her father became evasive. He managed a matter-of-fact tone, but his answer was dark and ominous.

"You know I have a gun."

Offering no further explanation, he rose from the table, leaving Esther to fill in the blanks of his cryptic revelation.

Chapter 3

The Trip

Paris, France | late January 2014

*T*he plane landed at Orly airport in the wee hours of the morning.

Itamar and Esther left the airport yawning in unison. They got on the bus and made their way to stay with Itamar's Aunt Jocelyn, the sister of his late mother. She lived in a three-story, brown residential building on the third floor. Itamar hesitated in front of the two doors before finally knocking on the left side.

His Auntie, short and round, opened the door for them. She looked at them with a smile through her round glasses. "I can't believe you're here!" she giggled, inviting them in.

They crossed the dark corridor. When they reached the living room, Esther sat down, exhausted, on the black leather sofa. Jocelyn pulled out a small red leather beanbag from under the living room table. She invited Itamar to sit down.

"So, what brings you here?" Jocelyn asked, sitting down next to Esther.

"We came looking for someone," said Itamar. His body threatened to engulf the little beanbag chair.

"We came looking for my birth mother." The words escaped from Esther's throat before she could stop them.

"So nice!" Jocelyn said, applauding. "You can tell me all about it. But first, let me order some sushi. You must be starving after your trip."

The food arrived and the conversation continued through dinner. Jocelyn listened, enthralled, as Esther and Itamar shared the story from beginning to end.

Jocelyn wished them "Good luck!" as both the meal and conversation ended for the evening. They went to bed, wondering what the next day would reveal.

∽

Itamar and Esther got up early the next morning and began their search. Arriving at the metro, the smells brought back memories Esther didn't realize she still had.

Their first stop was Italy Square, in the thirteenth arrondissement. It was where Esther was born. They made their way to the town hall.

"I need to have a birth certificate issued," Esther told Itamar as they walked to the escalator.

Ascending to street level, they blinked in bright daylight. "*How beautifully sunny,*" she thought.

The town hall building was old and impressive. There were stone arches with three blue wooden doors on the impressive building. Esther raised her head and examined the rows of windows placed at different heights. Some were placed above colorful flowerpots.

Several chimneys stood up from the black roof, under which a large dial clock was set. Esther wondered if they were still spewing smoke during the winter.

"Come, Esther," said Itamar.

The entrance hall was large and impressive in its beauty. Chandeliers hung from the ceiling. Pine poured over the statues placed throughout the space. A blue carpet covered the wooden staircase, and a railing made of wood and iron accompanied them.

"It looks like a royal hall," Esther said. Itamar smiled. They examined the signs and proceeded down a long corridor. At the end there was an office full of tables, gray iron cabinets, folders, and several government employees waiting for them.

"*Liberté, Égalité, Fraternité—Ville de Paris,*" said the posters spread here and there throughout the space.

Esther walked to the red plastic dispenser and ripped out a numbered ticket. They took a seat in chairs placed under portraits of the mayors going back several years.

After a lengthy time, a clerk called out, "Number 605, please!" Esther leapt out of her chair.

"I need a birth certificate please," she said as soon as she sat down in front of the clerk.

"ID, please." Esther presented her French passport. The clerk looked at it as his fingers simultaneously ran across the keyboard.

After a few moments, he got up, went over to the printer, and returned to them with a page in his hand. He picked up a stamp next to the computer, pressed it into the cushion of blue ink, stamped the document, and signed it.

"Here, Ma'am. Your birth certificate. You are welcome."

Esther took the document from his hand.

"Anything else?" the official asked. Esther examined the page. Five short lines were printed between the headline and the round stamp print. '*On 12 October 1974, she was born at 5:55 a.m. in the 13th arrondissement …*'

Further down the document, the names of Esther's parents, dates and places of birth appeared. She took a deep breath.

"Can I have my original birth certificate, please? I'm, uh, I'm adopted."

The clerk sighed. He looked at the chairs along the wall, which were full of people waiting. "I need to check with my manager," he said.

After a long time had passed, the clerk returned with another white sheet in his hand. He sat down and his body sank into the chair as if he were part of the table itself. "Please, ma'am. That's what we have. I was happy to assist."

'*Paris Municipality, Birth Certificate—Full Copy,*' was written on the top of the paper. '*On 11 May 1976, the court ruled …*'

She continued to read line by line until she reached her adoptive parents' names again.

"What is this?!" she asked the clerk. "Where's her name?"

"Whose name, Ma'am?" the clerk asked.

"My mother's name!" Esther replied in frustration. "What's the deal? You know her name, but won't share it with me?"

"French Law keeps your birth mother's identification protected," the official said. He began checking his watch.

"And what about me? Am I not protected?"

The clerk wrinkled his forehead. "I'm afraid I can't help you any further," he said. "Don't forget to take your passport, please."

"This is not fair!" Esther told him.

"Don't worry, babe. Everything is going to be okay." said Itamar.

"Let's get a coffee," Itamar said as they headed out into the sunlight again. "Look, there's a nice place there."

He pointed to a café across the road. Above it was a red sign with the words '*Café de France*.' They crossed the street. "*Brasserie-Restaurant 24/7*," read the awning painted in the colors of the French flag. "*Café - Vin - Limonade*."

Next to the round metal tables stood red and white straw chairs. Esther and Itamar went inside. A girl with long blonde hair, gathered in a ponytail, stood behind a long wooden counter. She wore a white apron and wiped a glass with it.

"Bonjour," she greeted them with a smile. Itamar ordered Esther a black coffee and a croissant and himself a hot tea. They drank quietly and watched people passing by.

"Why don't we go to the hospital where you were born?" said Itamar at last. "I'm sure they'll have more information there."

They left the café and walked to an enormous map of the city displayed on the corner of the street. Itamar ran his finger across the map until he found La Pitié-Salpêtrière Hospital in the 13th *arrondissement.*

They continued to line number 57 station and got on the bus. After nine-minutes, the driver signaled for them to get off at the next stop.

"Merci," said Esther as they came down.

The pedestrian entrance was a narrow path stretching to the right side of a small old building. It served as a gateway to the hospital.

"This place is massive," Esther commented. "And check out this garden. With all the flowers and statues, it's like a museum."

She approached a statue and read the inscription engraved at its base: '*Courage, Abstinence, Sacrifice.*' Chills ran down her spine.

An elderly man walked past them on a slow-walking path. Without the white cane on which he was leaning, his body would have folded in half.

"Sorry," said Esther, "Do you know where the maternity department is?"

The man giggled and then coughed. "I know where the geriatric department is," he said. "It's been many years since I've been in the maternity ward."

After wandering the building, they had finally found it. Esther stopped in front of the doors.

"Itamar," she said, pointing to the sign set above the door. "Maternity department, maternity department! Would you believe it? This is where me and my birth mom first met."

Her voice became sad. "And then she left me."

"Come on, baby. It's going to be okay." He pulled the heavy door open, but Esther didn't step forward.

"I'm scared," she said.

"Take a deep breath," Itamar said. "You're strong."

She followed him continuing down the hall until they reached the nurses' post.

"How can I help?" a woman in a green uniform asked them.

"Hello," said Esther. "I ... I was born here. Many years ago."

The woman smiled. "How many?"

"In 1974," Esther said.

"Nice," said the woman.

"And I am, uh, adopted," Esther said after Itamar shook his head and signaled for her to continue. "I'm looking for my birth mother."

"Oh, I get it," the woman said. "But all the files since then have been archived." the nurse added.

"But I need to find her," Esther replied desperately.

She examined the azure walls and the high windows. Next to one of them hung a calendar in a black pattern. Maybe if she concentrated enough, Esther thought, she could make it change back to 1974.

She turned to Itamar. "If I had come earlier, they would have found the file and I would have known her name," she said.

"It doesn't matter," Itamar replied. "Come on, we'll focus on what we can do now."

The nurse turned to them and said, "I have an idea. Can you wait for me for a moment?"

She left her post and disappeared into one of the back rooms. On the other side of the hall a glass door opened, and the metallic scent of blood burst out of it.

"Delivery room," said Esther, though there was nothing there confirming it. "Itamar, I was born right here," she said. "I've been here, you know? Right here."

Itamar grabbed her hand and led her to the waiting area. "Sit down for a minute," he said. "You're shaking."

Ten minutes later, the nurse returned to them. Esther saw a hint of sympathy in her gaze. It was an expression she recognized, and it gave her a stifling sense of disgust.

"Come on, let's go into the office for a minute," the nurse suggested.

Esther fought back the tears that insisted on streaming down her face.

"You know," smiled the nurse, "the midwife who worked here in 1974 still works here. She may even have been your birth mother's midwife."

"She may be the one who brought my birth mother and I together for the first … and possibly the last time," Esther told Itamar in Hebrew. She turned to the nurse. "Is she here?" she asked.

"No, I'm sorry," the nurse said. "She wasn't here today. She'll be here tomorrow if you want to come back. Regardless, I have the address of a place that might be able to help you."

She took a paper from the table adorned with the blue hospital logo reading '*Assistance Publique—Hôpitaux de Paris.*' She wrote something on the white page before handing it to Esther. "It's a charity the government has set up to help adopted children," she explained. "You've heard of the new law, haven't you? "

"No, I haven't," Esther said, sounding surprised.

"Recently, they passed a new law that will assist you in searching for your birth mother at no cost. They're likely closed by now, but tomorrow you can meet them in the morning."

Esther examined the page. The nurse's handwriting was beautiful and clear: '*Aide Social a l'enfance, 76-78 Rue de Reuilly, Paris 12 (Metro: Line 6 to Mongallet).*'

"Thank you, we will go there first thing in the morning" said Itamar.

As they headed out into the Paris streets, Esther turned around and looked at the hospital once more. "This is where I last saw her," she said.

Itamar and Esther did not wake up as early as they had planned. The toll of their journey from Israel and the exhaustive day spent searching for clues in Paris had left them fatigued. Itamar's aunt had graciously invited them for more sushi after the day's quest. They engaged in lively conversation lasting late into the evening.

Esther hadn't been able to fall asleep. She spent the night reflecting on the impact of her time at the hospital. It was where she had taken her first breath. She admitted to herself, "This is the first time I've felt close to her, even though she wasn't physically present."

The emotions that rose up from the search had created an unexpected feeling of intimacy. It was a feeling that transcended the physical distance and time since that pivotal moment in the hospital room.

The journey from Aunt Jocelyn's house to the 12th *arrondissement* was long. The walk from the station to the association's address was equally long. Several trees were scattered along the sidewalk. Their trunks were sooty from smoky exhaust.

Beyond fatigued, Esther sat down on a bench. A few seconds had passed, when Itamar called to her from across the road. "Esther, I found it! Come on."

They entered the building and took the elevator to the fifth floor. When the elevator door opened, a sign with the organization's name appeared in front of them. Underneath it was a black arrow pointing to the left.

They opened the door and found the office deserted. A moment later, a severe looking woman came out of an office in a tailored suit. "Hello, I'm sorry, but you'll have to come back later. All officials are on their lunch break."

"What do you mean, on a lunch break?!" erupted Esther.

Itamar put a hand on her shoulder. "When will they be back?" he asked the woman politely.

"At two. They're on their lunch break," the woman repeated.

"Thank you, we'll be back at 2:00," Itamar said. "Come on, Esther. We'll go down to get something to eat."

They walked a short distance before discovering a delightful area filled with a few busy restaurants during the lunch rush. Opting for a cozy bistro, they quietly waited for a table. They were seated facing a grand window that framed the lively street scene. Itamar placed their order—a chicken sandwich for himself and a salad for Esther.

"I can hardly swallow," she confessed as their food arrived. They ate in silence feeling the heavy weight of their emotions. They sat and watched the ebb and flow of people outside. It was a welcome respite from the search for clues about Esther's past.

At 1.55 p.m., Itamar opened the glass door to the office once again. This time, the serious woman did not come out to greet them. They sat down on chairs in the lobby and waited quietly.

"I'm sure they'll be back soon," Itamar said.

"What if she gave birth to me with sadness? What if she experienced difficulties?" said Esther. "You know, I'm not entirely sure I want to find out what ..."

"Hello!" interrupted an energetic young woman stepping out of one the inner offices. "How can I help you today?"

"We were given this address by the La Pitié Salpêtrière Hospital," Esther said, as she rose to her feet. "I'm adopted. I have a document here with a number that my adoptive parents gave to me. It's possible that this could be helpful."

She took out the document and handed it to the woman. The woman reviewed the document and said, "Let's go into my office. I'll give you a form, you can fill it out and we'll send you your file."

"That's it?" asked Esther.

"That's it," smiled the woman. "Since you were the property of the state of France, it will be easier for us to handle." she added.

Esther sat down at the table and took out a pen. There were only a few questions on the page.

'*Name before the adoption*'. Esther couldn't answer that one.

'*Name after the adoption*'. Esther wrote her name.

'*Date and place of birth*'. Esther filled in the details.

'*Case number*'. Esther searched the document she received from her mother. '*2896*,' she wrote.

'*Purpose of the request*'. Esther marked the relevant cube with an X: '*locating a biological mother*'.

She finished the form, requesting the file be sent to her address in Israel and signed it at the bottom of the page.

"Will the file contain my birth mother's name?" she asked the woman.

"First we'll have to find the file," the woman replied. "But no, her name will not appear in the file—the law protects her. I will give you the address and phone of another nonprofit that takes care of abandoned children. Once you receive the file, make a copy, and send the copy to them. They'll help you find her."

Esther nodded.

"Is there a payment required from me?" she asked.

"Of course not," laughed the woman with condescension in her voice. "We are a nonprofit for abandoned children. Don't be alarmed if the delivery takes some time. The files are archived, and it will take time to find them. But don't worry. We will find it and send it to you so you can proceed with the next step. Good luck!"

"What now?" asked Esther after they left the cold building and stood in the street.

"Now we'll go home and wait," Itamar replied and took her hand.

Esther and Itamar conveyed their heartfelt thanks and gratitude to Aunt Jocelyn before heading back to Israel. Once they touched down on familiar ground, they returned to their daily routines. But things were different. There was a palpable sense of anticipation lingering in the air.

As time passed, the uncertainty became more than challenging for Esther. She waited impatiently, yearning for the veil hiding her biological mother's identity to lift. Each passing day seemed to intensify her desire. The wait was excruciating. Her emotional journey continued.

Chapter 4

Life in an Envelope

The Western Negev, Israel | April 2014

"Mom, where are you going?" Esther's son inquired.
"To my parents' house," Esther responded.

"I want to go with you!"

"Not today," Esther said, bending down to speak to the boy. "Another time."

Her parents lived a short distance from her now. Esther walked the *kibbutz* paths to the small house. She recalled the day she first visited their temporary home three months ago:

"I see your couch, but where's all the other stuff?" Esther had asked nonchalantly.

Her father explained they had stored everything in boxes in another room to avoid renting a storage unit during the renovations. He then guided Esther through a room filled with stacked furniture and boxes before leading her to the bedroom where her mother was. She had proudly pointed out to Esther that her father had meticulously measured all their furniture to make certain it would fit.

It had been the start of what had become her daily routine.

She knocked on the stained white shutter door.

Her father greeted her with an enthusiastic "Welcome!" as she entered the compact space, it's walls adorned with a network of cracks.

"Cherie, Esther is here!" he joyfully declared, shutting the door behind her.

Esther's mother emerged from the bedroom, applauding. "Hello Esther, how are you doing?"

"Hey Mom, is there anything you need help with today?"

"I just need your help to get some things done in the kitchenette. We'll be fine until the renovation is finished," her mother assured. She grabbed Esther's hand, pulling her into the kitchenette. "Come on, your dad's going to bring the box with the glass plates. There's not much room anyway. There are only two cabinets and a small sink. Did you see that the washing machine is outside by the door?"

Esther's father entered the kitchenette with a large box. He placed it on the small table and turned to Esther.

"Esther, come see!" he exclaimed. "I'm sure you haven't seen it since we moved here. The toilet and shower are new."

Esther smiled and followed him while her mother opened the box, revealing clear glass plates and a few glasses.

"Look at this nice little kettle your dad bought us," she said to Esther when she returned. "Sadly, there's no room for our kettle here."

"Well, it's not for long, Mom," Esther comforted. "Have you met any people yet?" she asked. "Everyone's very nice here."

"To tell you the truth, Esther, I don't like community life. I miss my house."

"But you've been at the *kibbutz* for a while, Mom!"

Esther's mother sighed. "People keep asking questions about private things. It's not pleasant! They should focus on their own lives. I'm not used to it. I have a French mentality."

Esther left and went straight to her mailbox.

She nearly lost her breath when she discovered the notice inside. Since there was no post office in the *kibbutz*, packages and registered letters had to be picked up in the nearby town.

Esther rushed home to get her car keys, yelling, "I'll be back soon!"

She closed the door of her house and raced to her car. It didn't take long to drive to Ashkelon city.

The post office in the Barnea neighborhood was small. A white-red postal sign adorned the 'Lego cube' of a concrete building.

The back of the building gave the impression of abandonment, but upon opening the heavy glass door she discovered it was crowded with people. There was room on the one and only iron bench in the room.

Esther grabbed a numbered ticket and sat down. Time seemed to crawl by. Finally, it was her turn. She passed the notice she received to the clerk.

"ID," the man said without looking up from the counter. Esther passed him her ID, her hand trembling. He rose to his feet and made his way to the stack of boxes and envelopes in the corner of the room.

Esther waited with apprehension. He poked around in the pile and finally came back with a large beige envelope in his hand. Esther reached out, but he put the envelope next to him. "Sign here," he said.

Esther's hand trembled as she signed the forms, took the envelope, and left.

"Wait, ma'am, your ID!" the clerk exclaimed.

She grabbed the ID and ran outside.

Esther's hand plunged into her bag in search of the car keys. It took forever for her to find them and open the car door. She sat behind the wheel and examined the envelope. On one side was the black stamp of social services of the Municipality of Paris. Next to it was a bright blue stamp of the association. On the other side was a pink resin sticker of the French Post office.

She tore open the envelope and found a thick bundle of pages inside. Some of them had yellowed from age. Esther reviewed them, skimming a bit on every page before going back and reading them again. Finally, she set the pages on her knees. They slipped and fell to the floor of the vehicle. She bent over, picked them up, and took a deep breath.

At the top of the pile was an official letter from the association she had visited with Itamar.

'*Madame, per your request, your file is enclosed with this letter. Some documents have concealed information, as you will see. We did not send other documents as they pertain solely to your biological mother, who wished to remain anonymous and protect her privacy. You can request the removal of this confidentiality at the address below. Best regards and good luck.*'

Esther returned home and placed the envelope in her dresser. After dinner she put the children to sleep, then told Itamar she had received the file she had been waiting for.

She took the envelope from the dresser and treated it like a precious baby. Cautiously, she opened the envelope as Itamar stood silently beside her.

Arranging the pages on the dinner table, she reviewed them all. The birth certificate itself. The transfer certificate testifying that the staff of the hospital had entrusted it to the orphanage staff. The certificate testifying that on 22 May 1975 it was given to her adoptive parents.

She continued to read document after document until her eyes came across a name she didn't recognize: Frederique Anne Bertille.

She re-read the name once more. The letters were written with a steady hand and fine writing.

'*Frederique Anne Bertille was sent to the La Crèche Saint Vincent de Paul orphanage.*' It stated the girl was the Property of France. In addition to her name, she received an ID number.

Esther got up and grabbed a glass of water. She came back, sat down, and read the document from beginning to end once again. The name was her name. It had been given to her at birth in a Paris hospital. She breathed in deeply and closed her eyes.

Most of the other pages were status reports. Others were municipality paperwork that she didn't understand. She arranged them in piles, according to their topic: city documents, hospital documents, orphanage documents, etc.

When she finished reviewing the city documents, she moved on to the orphanage documents. A few months after her birth it was decided that the name Bertille would be used as her last name.

She went through the hospital papers. On the third page, she encountered lines of small handwriting. She thought it looked like the writing of a little girl, or someone ashamed of what she was about to do. She read the words. The tears began to flow. It was the first time she'd read her birth mother's handwriting.

'*I'm officially giving up my child, Frederique Anne Bertille, who was born on 12 October 1974. I wish to keep my name and my marital status a secret. I give my consent to give the child up for adoption by the choice of the welfare authorities. I understand the consequences of abandonment and that I have three months to change my mind.*'

Esther brought the form close to her eyes. Under the title '*Report of Abandonment (procès—verbal d' abandon)*' was written, '*I can't take care of the baby.*' The small print of the handwriting reminded her of the tiny legs of a fly.

She moved to the next page. The date written at the top of the document was 17 October 1974.

'*The biological mother kept the birth a secret from her family,*' the document said. '*Her partner of three years (1971) returned to Morocco. She noted that "he wouldn't have helped with the expenses, anyway." The father worked as a waiter at an undetermined restaurant. The biological mother, Mrs. ******* worked at the train station as a cleaner. She has another child from the same partner, and three children from previous relationships. The birth mother, Mrs. ********, adds that she "has no money to raise another child." She received the relevant information regarding her decision to hand over the newborn. Exterior appearance, mother: 157 cm, light hair, blue eyes, oval face, very light skin. Religion: Catholic, not traditional. Education: Schooling until the age of 15. Exterior appearance, father: 170 cm, black hair, brown eyes, brown skin. Religion: Muslim. Education: Unknown.*'

A different title was displayed at the top of the following page: *FRATRIE* (Siblings).

'*Paul was born in 1966. The eldest son of ******** from a previous marriage. Stayed at her ex-husband's parents' house when the mother went on her way.*'

'*Alain was born in 1968. Nadia was born in 1969. Both were taken to an orphanage as toddlers.*'

'*Two other newborns (1971) died during childbirth.*'

'*Malika was born in 1973 and remained in the mother's possession.*'

Thirty-tree pages summed up her life from birth to May 1975. Two hundred and twenty days, most of which she went through at the orphanage.

"Is that it?" Esther took the envelope and peered inside. A single photograph waited there, clinging to the corner of the envelope. It was a picture of a baby in a highchair, and behind it a window and a calendar.

She put the picture on the corner of the table and turned to the last stack of documents. There were letters from the court, a permit to leave the country, and pages that summarized the adoption process. At the bottom of one of them were the signatures of the adoptive parents, large and beautiful, next to their address in Paris. The house where she lived when she was a toddler.

Esther called to Itamar. "I have biological siblings," she said.

The following day Esther called the National Council for Access to Personal Origins.

"Please make a copy of your file and send us the copy. You can keep the original." A representative told Esther.

"You will need to attach a letter explaining that you're looking for your birth mother. When all this arrives, we'll start the search. We have investigators who are experts at this."

"Good," said Esther. "Thank you. How do I pay?"

"The French government has already taken care of it," laughed the woman across the line. Her tone changed to something more serious. "It's important for me to add that if your birth mother is deceased, God forbid, we won't be able to provide her name."

∞

"Our house renovation is taking forever," Esther's mother complained when Esther came to visit. "I want to return to my house."

"I'm glad you're only 5 minutes away from us. Isn't it delightful for your grandchildren to visit you on their bikes?" inquired Esther.

"Indeed, it is," Mom conceded. "But there isn't much to occupy us on the *kibbutz* except for waiting for the renovation to end."

Dad placed his hand on his wife's palm. "Would you like some tea?" he asked Esther. "Coffee?"

"Just water," Esther replied. She settled into a chair with her purse on her lap.

When her father returned from the kitchen, she pulled out an envelope. "Look at what I received from the nonprofit in Paris," she said.

"Nonprofit? What nonprofit?" her father inquired.

"For adopted children. You gave me the information to start my investigation, remember?" Esther clarified. "Inside the envelope is the information I've been searching for. So amazing, right? I got it in the mail yesterday, and I thought you would like to see it too."

Mom averted her eyes. "What for?" she asked. "I didn't understand why you went on this journey to look for her, and now I'm confused by this nonsense."

Esther's father shook his head and reached for the envelope. "Time has flown by," he chuckled as he perused the documents. "You know, Esther, it feels like we adopted you just yesterday." He flipped through the pages. "Look, here's your birth certificate!" he exclaimed. "Oh, and here are the details about the … Biological."

He brought the page closer to his eyes and read carefully. "The mother is a Catholic … all right … and the father …" He stood up abruptly. "What is this? Muslim?! It must be a mistake."

Esther's mother grabbed his hand, coaxing him to sit down. "Darling, what's gotten into you? Sit down and relax, please. It's not good for your health."

"It must be a mistake," her father repeated.

"How can that be a mistake?" asked Esther. "There's your signature and my picture here. Look. Is that not your signature? Isn't that me in the picture?"

Her father remained silent.

"Mom, say it," pleaded Esther. "What difference does it make if he was a Muslim?!"

"It doesn't matter," her mother declared, "because I'm your mother, and you don't have another mother, do you?"

Esther's father walked up to the window and peered into the scruffy little garden.

"I need to go out and mow the lawn," he finally said. "The neighbor owns a mower. I'm going to ask him if I can borrow it for a few minutes."

Esther watched him leave.

"Leave him; he'll be fine in a few minutes," Mom said. She took the TV remote, turned it on, and browsed through the channels until she found a cooking show on the French channel.

"See?" she said. "I told you, Esther, you're fortunate we're your parents! I don't know how you came up with that crazy idea to go searching. Your sister doesn't want to search for her birth mother. 'You're my mother, and I don't need another one,' she told me. Tell me if it's not true!"

"Yes, this is the undeniable truth. You are, and will always be, my mother," Esther whispered, a gentle sincerity in her voice. "I just felt the need to share this part of me with you."

Mom remained fixed on the television, the glow casting a soft light across her face.

Without diverting her gaze, she responded, "I didn't come across her name in any of your documents. I assumed that discovering her identity was the primary aim of all your research."

Esther leaned forward slightly. "Yes, her name was deliberately redacted. It appears the laws of France safeguard her, wrapped in a shroud of privacy that even my efforts couldn't pierce."

"Hmm, good for her," Mom remarked nonchalantly, her attention still on the TV screen. "Oh, look, Esther, the chef on the television is preparing the Black Forest cake you adore; La Forêt Noire."

Esther's mind swirled, caught up in the revelation of the new information and her routine everyday life.

Mom finally turned her eyes away from the screen, meeting Esther's gaze. There was a depth of understanding in her eyes. A silent acknowledgment of the complexity that life had thrown their way.

"Esther, my love," she said gently. "You've always been a part of our family, no matter where you came from. Biological ties are one thing, but the love and connection we share go beyond any piece of paper or secret kept in the shadows."

As Esther absorbed her mother's words, a profound sense of gratitude and warmth enveloped her. The noises of the TV show and the distant hum of everyday life outside seemed to fade into the background. The only thing left behind was a moment of profound connection.

Encouraged by her mother's acceptance, Esther delved deeper into her feelings. "I'm not sure where this journey will lead me, Mom. The search for my roots has opened doors to a past I never knew existed. But regardless of what I uncover, you will always be the heart of my story."

Mom's expression softened, a mixture of pride and reassurance. "Sweetheart, life is a journey filled with twists and turns. Embrace every step, and remember, no matter where your path leads, you'll always have a home here. Family isn't just about blood; it's about the ties we create. The love we share."

They sat in a shared moment of understanding, the unspoken bond between them strengthening. Esther and her mother found solace in the unbreakable threads of love that wove their lives together.

✍

"We found her!" declared a representative of the association in French, her voice resonating with excitement. "And it happened so quickly! You're incredibly fortunate!"

Esther's grip tightened on the phone as a mixture of excitement and anxiety overwhelmed her. She slowly sat down, the weight of the moment sinking in.

"So, she's alive?" she asked breathlessly. "She's not ... not dead, is she? What's her name? Where is she?"

"Yes, she's alive," came the reassuring response.

"What's her name?" Esther pressed on, her voice filled with a blend of hope and trepidation.

"We know her name and we have her address," the woman continued in a calm, measured tone. "But let me provide some context. She is an elderly woman ..."

Esther's breathing quickened, her emotions dancing on the edge of uncertainty.

"Ma'am, are you there?" the woman inquired.

"I'm here," Esther affirmed apprehensively.

"Alright," the woman continued. "As I mentioned, she's an older woman. We sent a social worker to talk to her, explaining that you were searching for her. She agreed to speak with you. That's good news, isn't it?"

"Yes," Esther replied, her relief evident. "Did she mention anything about me?"

"I'll check the social worker's records," the woman on the other end responded. "Can you hold a minute?"

"Of course," Esther replied, her gaze fixed on the wall as she waited anxiously for more information.

"Well, it's not the most pleasant news," the woman began again, her tone apologetic. "The truth is, she never actively sought to find you. The social worker had to remind her of who you were. As I mentioned, she's an older woman, and ..."

Esther interrupted, "Well, what's her name? Can you tell me where she lives?"

"Unfortunately, I can't provide you with her address just yet," the woman apologized. "I can only share that she resides near Paris."

"Near Paris," Esther echoed, her mind already racing with thoughts of what might come next.

"Yes. As I mentioned, she is open to you reaching out. Initially, it will be through a letter that you send to us, and we will forward it to her."

"I'm not sure what to write after so many years," Esther admitted, a mix of excitement and uncertainty in her voice.

"Write to her about yourself," the woman suggested, offering a guiding light in this new chapter. "Feel free to include pictures of your children. That's absolutely okay."

"Sure," said Esther, feeling a surge of gratitude for the woman's guidance. "I'll send the letter. Once you've had a chance to review its contents, please forward it to her. I'll include my phone number and address so we can continue the correspondence directly. Thank you so much." Esther's voice carried hope as she spoke.

"Good luck!" The woman bid her farewell.

As she hung up, Esther couldn't contain her elation.

"Itamar!" she cried out, "They found her! They really found her!"

"Who? What are you talking about, Esther?" asked Itamar, surprised by the sudden emotion in her voice.

"They found my birth mom," she said, her voice breaking as tears welled up.

"Wow, this is amazing. I'm so happy for you," Itamar said, enveloping Esther in a comforting hug.

Three long days passed before Esther mustered the courage to sit down at her desk to compose the letter. The blank page almost seemed to mock her.

After staring at it for several minutes, frustration gripped her and she wrote: "B-tch, b-tch, b-tch, b-tch." She crumpled the page, tossing it into the waste basket. Undeterred, she made another attempt: "B-tch, b-tch, b-tch." Again, the page met the same fate. A third try began with "Nasty b-tch."

Feeling discouraged, Esther moved away from her desk and walked into the living room where Itamar was watching TV. She settled beside him on the couch, sharing her internal struggle.

"The woman at the charity told me to write a letter so my birth mom would want to reach out to me," she explained. "She left me when I was only five days old, and now I'm expected to be nice to her, so she doesn't disappear again."

Itamar, sensing Esther's turmoil, lowered the volume of the television. "You really have nothing nice to say to her?" he inquired.

Esther sighed, grappling with conflicting emotions. "I don't know," she admitted.

"But thanks to her, you were born. Without her, you wouldn't exist," Itamar pointed out. "And in my eyes, it's very nice that you exist."

Taking his words to heart, Esther returned to her desk with a renewed perspective. Her next attempt at the letter began with a hesitant "Hello." She introduced herself as Esther, explaining that the nonprofit had suggested she write. Uncertain of what to say, she admitted, "Maybe I only want to tell you I understand you. And I forgive you."

On a separate page, she attached her phone number and address. She included several pictures capturing moments of her life with Itamar and their children. Each image told a story, a silent narrative of the life she had built, and the profound connections that now defined her.

"Hello?" A small voice at the other end of the line said in French. "Esther?" The voice hesitated. "It's me."

Esther was silent.

"Hello"' said the voice again. "It's me. Yvette."

Esther sat down on the rocking chair next to the window. It was the first time she had heard the voice, yet it sounded oddly familiar. It was the first time she had heard her name. Her heart broke.

"Hello," she replied in French. "Do you want me to call you back? What's your number? The calls from France to Israel are expensive, I think."

"Yes, please," Yvette said.

Esther reached for the notebook next to the phone and hastily wrote down the number.

"I'll call you back right away," she said.

She immediately returned the call. When their conversation was finished, Esther hung up the phone and burst into tears. That's how Itamar found her when he came home hours later.

"Is everything okay?" he asked. "Why are you sitting like this in the dark?"

"She called," Esther said. "My mother."

Itamar panicked. "I thought she was here with the kids this afternoon."

"Not her," Esther clarified. "My biological mother. She called a minute after Mom walked out the door. As soon as she closed the door, the phone rang. My God. Just think what would have happened if she had been here when the phone rang." She burst into nervous laughter.

"So how was it?" asked Itamar, placing his bag next to him on the floor.

"I don't know," Esther said. "She was very nice and polite. She asked me for the kids' birthdays. She called them her grandchildren. Can you believe that? But she didn't remember MY birthday. And she was there!"

"Well, she's an older woman," Itamar said.

"I would love to meet her in person," Esther said.

"We'll need to wait a little while. It's a lot to process for you and for her" Itamar said gently.

"I have waited all my life to meet her!" Esther cried.

"Yes, I know, and you will I promise." Itamar kissed her on the cheek.

Esther opened her eyes in the dark bedroom. She couldn't sleep. The digital clock on the nightstand showed it was 3 am. She rolled over on her back and tried to guess the distance between herself and the ceiling.

She replayed the conversation with Yvette in her mind, hoping she hadn't said anything bad.

"Where's Yvette now?" She asked herself. "She must be lying in the dark, too, lonely." Her heart shrunk.

The waiting lasted for two weeks until Yvette's first letter arrived.

July 17 from Saint Cloud

*'Dear Esther, I received your first letter with
the pictures of the children. I was happy to
hear from you. I read in the letter that you're
back in school, and I hope it's a success. Like
you, I am also a big fan of animals, especially
cats. It's a love that means a lot to me. I love
taking pictures. I also read a lot and watch TV.
I'm attaching some pictures, one of me and
some of my house. Soon I'll be sending more
pictures and will write to you again. I hope
your husband and kids are okay. Hope you're
okay, too. Sending kisses to you and your little
family, Yvette Ribono.'*

Esther, waving the letter, shared the contents with Itamar.
"Look, Itamar," she exclaimed. "She likes to read like I do,
and she loves cats and taking pictures, too!"

Esther examined the attached pictures. One featured
a green shrub from Yvette's garden. Others displayed
snow-covered trees and a fence. She couldn't help but be
drawn into the narrative Yvette was sharing. The last photo
showed an aged image of Yvette on a bridge. The colors
were faded, and her features were barely discernible.

"What do you mean, you wrote her a letter?!" Esther's mother said, enraged. "You don't know her. What did you even have to say to her?"

Esther's father walked into the kitchen showing an expression of annoyance. "Why are you being so loud?" he asked. "What happened? What are you arguing about?"

"Please repeat what you just said, Esther," her mother ordered before turning to her husband. "Darling, you should sit down."

"They found her," Esther said. "She's alive."

"Who? What are you talking about?"

"She's talking about her birth mother," her mother said. "You know, Esther, maybe she won't want to talk to you. You should honor her wishes to remain unknown. There's nothing that can be done."

Esther paced the small kitchen space, wondering how best to handle the topic.

"Mom, everything's fine," she said. "I wrote to her, and ..."

"Can you start over, please?" her father asked.

"Well," said Esther. "You remember I sent my file to the nonprofit, yes?'

"What?!" her mother revolted. "Why did you send them your file? I hope you made a copy of it first!"

"Yes, Mom," smiled Esther. "I made a copy of the file and sent them the copy along with my request."

"Well, good," her mother said without looking at her.

'The association searched and found her. They have private detectives," Esther continued.

"I hope you didn't pay too much, Esther," Mom said. "You don't need ... unnecessary expenses."

"I didn't pay, Mom. After they found her, I wrote her a letter and she answered."

"Wait," said her mother, rising from her chair with a frown. "When did all this happen?"

"Over the past few weeks," Esther said. "Maybe it's been a couple months. I don't know. It's been a while."

"And you didn't tell us?" Mom said.

Esther shrugged and said nothing.

"But I'm your mother, aren't I?" asked Mom with tears in her eyes.

"Sure, Mom," Esther said. "But it's not about you."

"You know, Esther," her mother continued, "When you were 18 and wanted to find your birth mother, we did everything we could."

"Of course, I know that."

"Then I'll tell you something," Mom said continuing on. "Before, I didn't want to tell you so that you wouldn't worry about me, but during this time I had diarrhea every day. For five weeks, that's how it was every day. And do you know why?"

Esther shook her head.

"It's because of the shock," Mom said. "It's because I convinced myself that you're my child from my womb. I forgot you were adopted. Strange, isn't it? You may remember Mrs. Sultan. I was at her place in therapy. That's what she told me then: that I forgot I wasn't your birth mother. That's what it's like when you love with all your heart." She paused and took a sip of water. "And your father, he had nettle rash all over his body. It's a skin disease, you know. And it's very itchy. He didn't sleep at night for a week, poor thing. Tell her."

Esther's father adjusted his *kippah* on his head. "Let her talk. Why are you even saying any of this?" he said.

He turned his attention back to his daughter. "Keep going, Esther."

"That's it," Esther concluded. 'The association found her and connected us and that was it."

"So, tell me a little about her," her mother commanded. "What did you talk about? What is her name? How old is she, and where does she live?"

"She's 73, Mom …"

"So younger than me," her mother noted with disappointment. "About your father's age. Well, that's nice."

"Yes," said Esther. "I have something else to tell you. Itamar and I want to fly to meet her in person."

"Why?" asked Mom. "When?"

"Next week," said Esther. "Itamar has already taken time off from work. If you could help me with the kids … It's going to be a short trip."

"I don't understand what's so urgent," Mom said.

Esther cleared her throat. "She's already an old woman," she began, "and I'm a little scared that…"

"She's younger than me," her mother interrupted. "And besides, our renovations will finish soon. We need to go back home. I've been waiting for this for months. I thought you could help me pack."

"I thought it was already packed," Esther said. "In the room over there. There are only few things from the kitchen and some clothes. Two boxes worth, I think."

"Yes, you must be right," Mom said. "But I'm your mother, right, Esther?"

"Sure, Mom."

"Well, fine. How long is this trip? Poor kids. Last time it was very difficult for them, you know."

"Two or three days, nothing more," Esther said. She stood up and put a hand on her mother's back. 'Thank you, Mom. I hope you're okay."

"Yes, I'm fine, Esther. I'm a responsible woman. And you're a responsible adult, too."

She rose from her chair.

"Well, now I have to make dinner for your father. And I have a lot more to organize. Goodbye." It was her way of ending the topic and dismissing Esther.

"Goodbye, Mom," Esther said, kissing her cheek. "And goodbye, Dad."

"Goodbye," said her father. "Good luck."

Chapter 5

She Looks Just Like Me

Saint-Cloud, France | August 2014

*E*sther found herself once again in the living room of
Aunt Jocelyn's house, delicately sipping her coffee.
She placed her cup down carefully on the table. She wanted
to avoid any accidental stains on the festive white shirt
she had chosen. She thought it added a touch of elegance
to her appearance.

Itamar, sensing her anxiousness, reassured her, "You
don't need to rush with the coffee. I'll call us a cab. We'll
definitely be on time."

When the cab arrived, Itamar provided the driver with
the address in Saint Cloud. The anticipation of the meeting
loomed in Esther's mind during the seemingly endless ride.
She wished, for a fleeting moment, that the journey would
stretch on indefinitely. The scheduled lunch meeting with
Yvette was set for noon.

"Maybe she won't even show up," Esther remarked nervously to Itamar.

She wiped sweat from her face. The day was oppressive;
hot and humid.

"She'll come; you don't have to worry. We will be there in a moment," Itamar reassured her.

Esther placed a hand on her chest, feeling a sudden pang of heartache.

The streets of Paris passed by the window; a sight Esther missed dearly. Driving school, pharmacies, department stores—familiar landmarks filled her with nostalgia.

As they entered the wide Boulevard de la Republique, Esther peered through the front window. Near the entrance of a restaurant, an elderly woman with blonde hair stood waiting.

"I see her!" Esther exclaimed. "Stop!"

The cab halted near the sidewalk.

"I've never seen her before, but I recognize her," Esther whispered.

An internal debate raged within Esther about their impending greeting.

"What should I do, Itamar?" she questioned, hesitant to open the taxi door. "Kiss her? Maybe just shake hands? We don't even know each other."

"I don't know. Just go," Itamar advised.

The woman, like Esther, wore a white shirt.

"Hello, Yvette." Esther greeted her quietly as they approached. "Is that you?"

Yvette turned, visibly embarrassed and pale. It seemed to Esther she was looking around to make certain no one was watching.

"Hello. Yes, it's me," Yvette responded, rushing up to Esther and kissing her on both cheeks.

"Very nice to meet you," Itamar added, extending his hand. The trio stood frozen, rigid as iron bars.

"Come," Yvette broke the silence. "I'd like to invite you to lunch."

They entered the restaurant. The waiter greeted Yvette as 'Mrs. Ribono,' leading them to a corner. The walls seemed to swirl around Esther. "This is my regular spot," Yvette explained. "Order whatever you want. It's my treat."

"I just want a salad," Esther replied, barely able to breathe. She gazed out the window as she ate her meal, lost in her thoughts.

Once they had finished lunch, they found themselves standing on the sidewalk again.

"I live here, right across the street," Yvette said. She pointed to a modern, yellow, six-story building adorned with colorful flower plants on the balconies.

Esther looked at the building, unsure of what to say. "Exquisite," she finally uttered.

"Well, come on, we'll go to my place," Yvette suggested. "I bought some snacks so we could celebrate the reunion."

Esther stood surprised. She thought the reunion was over.

"Thank you for the invitation," she said. "That's very nice of you."

Yvette smiled. "It's nothing!"

"Yes," Esther said. "I mean, sure, we'd love to go up, right, Itamar?"

She turned toward the building entrance before Yvette could change her mind. They walked along a wide path bordered by rose bushes. The sign above the front door proclaimed, *LES JOURS HEUREUX*—'Happy days'.

Yvette pointed to the mailboxes. "This is where I got your first letter," she revealed.

As they entered the small studio apartment, Esther complimented Yvette on the arrangement. "It looks very nice, Yvette," she said politely. "I see you also have a TV in here."

"Yes," Yvette replied. "We have a room with a TV downstairs as well, but I'd rather watch it alone in my room."

"That's good," Esther remarked.

"Yes, I love watching TV, reading, and I love the cats down in the backyard. But I've already told you this in my letters."

To the right stood a small single bed that resembled a little girl's bed. Esther looked at the other adornments in the room: a piggy bank, a tray with a red-striped glass bottle, a blue painting in a red frame, and a drawing of fishermen's ties on a small wooden dresser. Long white curtains covered the wide window.

"Only in France can you find such beautiful curtains," Esther whispered to Itamar, blushing. "My mom has the same."

A few, low black plastic tables, adorned with potted plants, stood under the window.

"This is where I put my Christmas tree," Yvette said, pointing there. "My apartment is small, but it's better than nothing. Please ... sit."

As they settled around an oval table covered by a white tablecloth, Yvette shared stories about the furniture and decorations. The room contained a bottle-green armchair, a shiny gilded clock on one wall, and shelves filled with books in French. Portraits hung on the wall opposite Esther. One displayed a forest scene, another a flower jug photo. There were three personal photos—one of two girls, another of an elderly woman, and a third of a young man in uniform.

A sudden realization struck Esther. A few weeks ago, she did not know of her birth mother, her name, or even if she was alive. Now she found herself amidst Yvette's personal and intimate belongings.

"I'll get us something to drink," Yvette said, heading towards the kitchenette.

"We look so much alike that it's scary," Esther whispered to Itamar. "Have you seen it? We share the same facial features, same eye color, same nose, and same mouth. It's so weird. All my life I've been looking for who I look like and now ... it just doesn't seem real. It's like seeing myself older."

Yvette returned with a tray holding a bottle of Champagne, glasses, and a saucer filled with cubes of cheese.

"Itamar, what do you do?" Yvette inquired as she sat down. "I mean, what is your occupation, if I may ask?"

Esther half listened to Itamar's response while her mind wandered.

"I read in my file," Esther interjected suddenly.

"What?" asked Yvette.

"In the file they sent me in Israel," Esther clarified. "There was a lot of information. I understand you've had a hard time. I'm not angry."

"Yes," Yvette sighed. "I used to clean at a train station, and I didn't have any money. It's a good thing social services gave me this apartment."

"It's very nice here, and you've arranged everything nicely," Esther praised. "But my file didn't have all the information. Can you tell me what happened before I was born, maybe? Please?"

Yvette fell silent. Esther downed the contents of her champagne glass.

"I was born in Bretagne in the north of France," said Yvette, turning her gaze to Itamar.

"Oh wow, that's where my parents took me for vacation when I was a little girl. We went to Carnac in Bretagne often," Esther smiled.

"My mom was engaged and pregnant with me, but her fiancé ran away just a few hours before they were to be married." Yvette looked down at the floor. "At that time, it wasn't appropriate for a woman to be pregnant and unmarried. I think it was the people in her community who arranged for her to marry a man whose wife had just died. He was a widower with lots of young kids. At that time, it wasn't acceptable for a man to be left alone with small kids to take care of. So, my mom and that man were married, and a few weeks later, I was born."

"When I was old enough, they started to use me as their slave. I had to do all the household chores, the laundry, and the cooking. I received orders from my mom's husband, and then from his kids ... even from my mom. So, when I was 18, I ran away to Paris and started a new life. It was hard."

Yvette stopped talking; her face was red.

"Thank you for sharing. What about when you met my father? What about all my siblings?" Esther couldn't hold herself back any longer.

Yvette did not reply immediately. Instead, she got up and went to the bookcase, returning with pictures in a green frame. "That's your sister Malika," Yvette said. "She's a year older than you. She looks like your father. When I was pregnant with you, he left me alone with her. Just like that, alone with a little girl, and he went back to Morocco."

She placed the picture in front of Esther, just out of reach. "If I had known, I would have kept you and given her away. You look like me. You're beautiful. You have a good heart and a normal life."

Esther shrunk at the revelation.

"Should we go for a walk?" suggested Itamar. "It's a beautiful day outside."

Esther stood up, eager to leave the small apartment.

"Wait," Yvette said. "I want us to take a picture together, to have a souvenir."

Itamar captured several photos of them standing side by side, yet not touching.

"Before you leave, I have a few things to give you, Esther," Yvette said. "Come with me for a minute."

Esther followed her to a white door set in one wall.

"I didn't buy you anything," Yvette said, "but I have some things here that I want to give you."

"No, it's okay," Esther protested. "I didn't buy you anything either."

"You need to keep your money," Yvette insisted. "You have children and a husband, and you paid for the flight to come here. That's enough."

Yvette opened the pantry door, revealing cramped shelves filled with an assortment of items. Yvette handed Esther a brown reindeer doll, explaining it was for her little one from her grandmother. She followed up with a pillow, serving as both a blanket and a teddy bear, for another of Esther's kids.

"Thank you," Esther said, her hands now laden with various items. Along with the children's items, Yvette gave Esther a rectangular wooden box, a cake spatula, plastic boxes, cloth napkins decorated with red flowers, and salt and pepper shakers. Yvette handed her a plastic bag to carry the items.

They all walked out of the small apartment together, taking the elevator to the ground floor. Yvette warned Esther about the building manager. She explained they needed to keep their relationship a secret. She didn't want to jeopardize her subsidized living arrangements by admitting she had children.

When they reached the lobby, there stood the building manager.

"Oh, hello, Madame Ribono! How are you today? Having company?"

The manager, a woman, in her forties with black hair and black eyes, looked at Itamar, who offered a smile in return.

"Esther, this is the manager of our wonderful establishment," Yvette introduced, gesturing towards the woman.

"Nice to meet you. Wow, she looks like you; this is crazy," said the woman, smiling at Esther.

Yvette turned to the manager. "This is my niece. She came to visit from Israel. It's just a brief visit." Yvette smiled as she responded with the lie.

Esther and Itamar courteously replied and headed to the front door of the building.

Leaving the building, they turned left onto the wide boulevard where they had first met.

"Sorry, Esther," Yvette apologized after a prolonged silence.

"What about?" Esther asked, attempting to keep her voice casual.

"I told the building manager you were my niece," Yvette said. "I don't have a choice, you know? This nursing home receives subsidies. If they knew I had kids, they'd throw me out of there."

"It's okay," Esther reassured her. She turned back to look at Itamar, who was trailing behind.

"So, you're a Christian?" Esther inquired after walking in silence for a while. Yvette waved her hand. "Yes, but I'm not doing anything with it. Not going to church. I don't care."

"It's a shame," Esther lamented. "I'd actually like to do Christmas, but I can't."

"Why?" Yvette questioned.

"Because … I mean, I'm Jewish," Esther admitted. "My family doesn't do that kind of thing. But I like churches. You really don't go there on Sundays?"

"No," Yvette replied. "I don't like churches."

"I do," Esther confessed again, this time with disappointment. She had hoped to find a common theme for conversation with Yvette.

"So do you have friends in this nursing home?" she asked.

"Yes, I have a few," Yvette replied. "Sometimes we do activities together, but they are all old. Sometimes they die. It's not a fun thing, being in a nursing home."

"I understand," Esther said. She gathered her courage to broach another topic. "What about Malika? Can I talk to her?" she asked.

"No," Yvette said bluntly. She quickly changed the subject. "Look, what a beautiful building! You don't have any like these in Israel, do you, Esther?"

"No," Esther confirmed. "I miss the beauty of Paris."

They continued walking, exchanging glances.

"It's getting late," Itamar intervened. "We need to get back to my aunt's house."

"I'll escort you to the Metro," Yvette offered.

As they reached the Metro station, Itamar left them to buy their tickets. Esther and Yvette stood in the pavilion, not talking nor looking at one another. Time seemed to stand still.

An elderly woman in a glowing vest approached them with a broom in hand. "Bonjour, Madame," she greeted Yvette. "Who is this, your daughter? How beautiful she is! She looks just like you!"

"Yes," Yvette said proudly, surprising Esther with her response. "This is my daughter."

Esther's breath caught in her chest, and tears welled up in her eyes.

During the trip back to Aunt Jocelyn's house, Esther remained silent, staring at the bag filled with seemingly trivial items from Yvette. The words she had said echoed in her head: "Yes, that's my daughter."

"How are you feeling?" Itamar asked, hugging her.

"I'm not sure," answered Esther with a small voice.

"It's good that you met her, right?" he asked.

"Yes, I'm happy, but it's a lot to process. She was nice but shared very little, so I'm confused," Esther explained.

"I'm sure it wasn't easy for her either. She is old and looked confused and overwhelmed," Itamar said.

"Yes, I know. I tried not to push her too much, but I've waited for that moment all my life. That might have been my only chance."

"I know, but it's nice she agreed to meet you and made a big effort." Itamar smiled.

"Can you imagine looking for someone who looks like you your whole life? When I was young, I was on the Metro." She looked towards the train station. "I was looking for someone with the same hair color and blue eyes. Despite the crowded train, I felt alone. Whenever I saw someone, especially women, with blue eyes, I wondered if we were related."

Itamar took her hand.

"You are not alone anymore, and now you know her," he said calmly.

"She looks just like me," Esther smiled.

"You look just like her," Itamar corrected.

Near the end of the evening, she called Yvette from Aunt Jocelyn's house.

"Tomorrow afternoon we're flying back," she said. "Is it okay if I stop by your house to say goodbye on our way to the airport? It will only take a minute, and I'm going to come alone."

"I'm sorry," Yvette replied politely, "but it's impossible." "Have a pleasant flight." She said with a calm voice and hung up the phone.

Chapter 6

How Are You, Darling?

Ashkelon, Israel | September 2014

The trip to her parent's home took longer than Esther remembered. It was a strange feeling. The months since her parents had lived within walking distance of her had dimmed in her memory. A container full of building debris sat at the end of the street. Remnants of their finished home renovation.

Esther noticed the changes. A whitened concrete wall had replaced the old fence around the yard. The wild bush that grew there in the past was gone. A modern iron gate had replaced the dilapidated wooden gate. Esther pressed the little bell and smiled at the camera lens installed next to it. She heard a buzzing sound, and the gate opened. The walking trail was smooth and comfortable. There was no sign of the dismantled parking shed nor the jammed stairs. There was also no sound of her dad's familiar footsteps.

The yard was an oasis full of new plants. The front door was replaced and remained closed. Mom's habits hadn't changed with the renovation. The kitchen door, however, was wide open and beautifully painted. "Welcome!" cried Mom from the doorway.

Esther came in and looked around. The ceiling, walls, and floor were all smooth and white. A narrow row of new white cabinets replaced the broken doors that had once formally held space there. Only the round marble table and the two black chairs remained as they had been.

"Wow, this is stunning!" said Esther. "Congratulations!"

"Thank you," smiled Mom. "Let's go, I want to show you around the house."

Mom opened a heavy metal door and flipped the light switch. A neon bulb stuttered on the ceiling. "We added a safe room, you see?" she said. "It was very dangerous here before, with the security situation. I'm putting in yours and your sister's beds. They are from England. They're gold, do you remember? And in the middle of everything is the commode. What can I do? I don't have the space to have it in my room anymore."

Dad's study at the end of the hallway was filled with boxes next to a full laundry rack.

"What a mess!" sighed Esther's mother. "What can I do?"

When they got to the bedroom, her mother's face lit up.

"And this is our room," she declared happily. "We now have a shower, toilet, and ceiling-high closet."

On the side of her father's bed stood the old nightstand; its glory appeared diminished in the renovated room.

When they finished the tour, Esther sat down in the kitchen and touched the edge of the fruit bowl.

"So, Esther, how was France?" her mother finally asked. "I know it's been a while since you went, but you haven't spoken about it."

"It was fine, Mom. I didn't want to bother you with it while you were moving back into your house."

"Well, are you ready to share what happened now? Tell me more. You came here to tell me. Right, Esther?"

"Nothing special happened. We had lunch with her and took a short walk afterwards. That's it."

Mom went to the sink and filled a glass of water. "Does she look like you, Esther?" mom asked.

"Do I look like her, you mean?"

Esther's mother took a pink pill and swallowed it with a big sip of her water.

"Yes," Esther finally said. "I look a lot like her."

"But it doesn't matter," her mother said. "Right, Esther? I'm your mother."

"Yes, Mom. You're my mother."

"So, fine," her mother said. "Well, now tell me. Where did you meet? Are you still in touch? Do you have a picture of her? How old is she? I remember you told me, but I can't remember how old she is."

"Her name is Yvette, and she's seventy-three," Esther said. "She's got blue eyes."

"So, she told you what happened to her? Why did she put you up for adoption?" her mother asked.

"She was alone raising another little girl. Her partner left, and she was a cleaning lady on the trains. She didn't have any money. That's all."

"You know, Esther, you were so cute when we got you," Mom said, and sat down next to her. "I was completely shocked. The shock made me cry for an entire week. I lost eight kilos, you know? And I wasn't fat, anyway. I always asked myself how anyone could leave a child like that. That's not possible."

Esther's father had come into the room earlier and had been listening to the conversation. He stepped forward and softly laid a hand on her back.

"So, was it hard?" he asked.

"Yes, Dad. But it's over." Esther whispered.

"Did you at least get all the answers you were looking for?" Her father asked.

"Not really." Esther shrugged and changed the subject.

"I love your house now that the renovations are finished. It's so much easier to move around without too many steps inside," Esther exclaimed.

"Yes, we even got rid of the stairs in the yard. They were way too dangerous for your mom," added Dad.

"We waited until we had the money from your grandmother, Dad's mom. After she passed, your father and his siblings sold the house, and we got our share. That's how we could afford the renovation," Mom explained in a serious tone.

"I was so happy when you were living near me. The kids were thrilled to visit you after school. I thought you were going to sell your house in Ashkelon and buy a house in the kibbutz," said Esther.

"Esther, seriously, we're way too old to move again, and we love our house," said Dad.

"I want to enjoy the renovations of our home," added Mom.

Her mother got up from the table and walked into the living room. When she returned, she held an old photo in her hand. She put it on the table in front of Esther.

"May 22, 1975," Esther's mother said. "That's the day we got you. I remember it like it was yesterday. We'd been waiting for you for so long! The weather was nice, and I was wearing a white leather jacket and floral skirt. You know it; it's the bright skirt with the pink flowers. I approached you slowly. I was afraid you'd start crying. You seemed so sad to us. This is a picture of you. Your eyes were filled with hopelessness and loss. You look so sad—it's been in my heart until now. It was horrible. But we were happy to meet you finally in person. I don't understand how anyone could leave such a sweet girl."

Esther looked down at the photo. The baby in the photo seemed to gaze back at Esther.

"How are you, darling?" Mom asked.

Esther smiled and looked up at her mother.

With a contented sigh of finality she responded, "I'm home."

A Note from the Author

*W*hen I think about my journey writing *You Are Allowed*, I realize it wasn't solely about my adoption. While crafting my memoir, I transitioned from the voiceless infant given up for adoption to an empowered woman who proudly declares, "I'm Odelia, and I am allowed."

"You Are Allowed" was the name of a chapter in my first manuscript that I wrote nearly a decade ago. This chapter did not appear in the final manuscript that was published in 2021 but became the title of the book. For me, it symbolized the shedding of limitations, allowing *You Are Allowed* to emerge. This poignant title gave me the freedom to shape and share my story authentically.

This journey has led me from the shadows of victimhood to a better understanding of motherhood; not just as an adoptee but as a mother myself. Speaking the words "I'm adopted" at age 45 marked a personal triumph. It signaled the acceptance of my identity and the embracing of my unique narrative.

It also allowed me to get to know my mom as a woman and not just as my mother. She was an exceptional woman. This realization influenced me in how I would mother my own children. She, too, was impacted by her own mother, and the generational influence was profound. I made a conscious decision to break the cycle and change my approach to parenting.

After publishing the first edition of **You Are Allowed**, I had an exceptional conversation with my mom. It was a conversation I had wished for my entire life. We finally understood each other without presumption and circumstance. This unexpected connection brought a deeper level of healing and closure. It bridged the emotional gaps that had persisted for years.

In this transformative odyssey, forgiveness, love, and respect emerged as guiding principles. As you read these last pages, I invite you to remember that YOU are allowed to navigate your own narrative with courage, compassion, and the liberating force of self-acceptance.

The freedom to express oneself through writing is a powerful tool. It not only allows personal discovery, but also invites others to embark on a similar journey. While it may be a difficult path, the challenges encountered during this process are essential for personal growth and self-awareness.

Your story is not isolated. As you dig into the pages of your own experiences, remember that you play a unique role not only in your individual story, but also in the broader story of existence. Your voice, your struggles, and your triumphs contribute to the rich and complex narrative of humanity.

Knowing your story can provide you with clarity on how you want to live your life. By exploring the depths of your experiences and understanding the threads that weave your narrative, you gain insight into your values, passions, and aspirations. This self-awareness becomes a compass, guiding you toward a life that aligns with your authentic self.

I encourage you to embrace the difficulty, moments of uncertainty, and the profound introspection that writing brings. By doing so, you not only reclaim your voice but also become an active participant in the ever evolving and interconnected story of creation. Each word you write adds to the collective expression of the human experience. It creates a tapestry weaving together the threads of countless individual stories into something greater than us.

Forgive yourself first.
Love yourself first.
Respect yourself first.
You are allowed.
~Odelia

If you've enjoyed this book and found a piece of yourself within the pages, I would love to connect to hear your OWN story of self-acceptance and transformation. I encourage you to connect. Send me an email at *OdeliaElgarat@gmail.com*

Should you wish to create your own legacy through writing, or would like to explore other ways to work together professionally, you may either email me or visit my website: *www.odeliaelgarat.com*

Glossary

Kibbutz- A communal settlement in Israel largely centered on agriculture.

Aliyah- the process of immigration and obtaining citizenship and residency in the home state of Israel.

Rabbinate- An institution for the Jewish community and office of those holding the position of a Rabbi.

Shabbat- Jewish day of rest. It is the seventh day of the week in Judaism (Saturday).

Bourekas- Pastries made from thin, hand-stretched dough, like filo or yufka, and stuffed with ground meat, cheese, spinach, eggplant, or a combination thereof that are popular on the Jewish dairy holiday of Shavuot.

Chevra Kadisha- An organization of Jewish men and women who see that the bodies of deceased Jews are prepared for burial according to Jewish tradition. They protect the bodies from desecration, willful or not, until burial.

Kippah- A brimless cap made of cloth worn by Jewish males to fulfill the customary requirement that the head be covered.

Minitel- A French online service accessible through telephone lines which was the world's most successful online service prior to the World Wide Web.

Moshav- A type of Israeli town or settlement, particularly a cooperative agricultural community of individual farms.

Mezuzah- A small folded or rolled parchment inscribed by a qualified calligraphist with scriptural verses to remind Jews of their obligations toward God.

Arrondissement- A district or subdivision within the city of Paris, France.

Acknowledgments

*I*n extending my heartfelt acknowledgments, I find it necessary to express my deepest gratitude to Assaf Schur, a literary editor of unparalleled dedication, who has been my steadfast companion throughout the years. Assaf, your boundless patience and sensitivity have been a guiding light. You are an unwavering presence that has breathed life into my words and stories. Your belief in my abilities persisted even when I faltered at times, making our collaborative journey an utterly transformative and life-changing process. I don't have the words to express the profound impact of our collaboration.

A special note of appreciation goes to Oded Wolkstein, a dear soul whose encouragement and warm words about the manuscript served as a wellspring of inspiration. Your generosity and support have helped to shape the narrative. I am profoundly grateful for your presence on this literary odyssey.

Omri Herzog, your remarkable ability to create an environment where authenticity knows no bounds has provided me with the freedom to be unequivocally myself. Your influence has been pivotal, fostering an atmosphere where creativity and expression thrive without constraints. I extend my deepest thanks for your invaluable contribution to the journey.

Nurit Gertz, a beacon of wisdom and love in the realm of writing. I owe you a debt of gratitude for your teachings and the courage you instilled in me to embark on this creative endeavor. Your insights have been a guiding force, shaping the essence of my work.

To Sheral DeVaughn for her editing prowess. You have breathed life into the English edition of my book. I sincerely appreciate you. Your meticulous work and dedication to preserving the integrity of the narrative are truly commendable.

A heartfelt thank you to Veronica Yager for her indispensable role in the book's production and seamless transition to an English-speaking audience.

Thank you to Gary Barnes for your love and support during this amazing journey.

To my husband, Sharon, I am continuously reminded of your unwavering support and love. They have been constant companions, especially during the most challenging times. Your encouragement has been my pillar of strength, and I am deeply thankful for your presence on this journey.

To my children, Danielle, Yuval, Shanni, and Erez. Your tireless support and encouragement have been the driving force behind this creative expedition. Each of you has contributed to the tapestry of this narrative in your own unique way.

A special mention to my eldest daughter, Danielle, whose breathtaking painting of me as a child encapsulates the very essence of the tumultuous journey I have undertaken. Your artistic expression adds a profound layer of meaning to the work, and I am genuinely moved by your talent and creativity.

In gratitude and appreciation.

www.ingramcontent.com/pod-product-compliance
Lightning Source LLC
Chambersburg PA
CBHW060509130626
46553CB00002B/437